THE MURDER GUIDE
TO GREAT BRITAIN

THE MURDER GUIDE TO GREAT BRITAIN

Geoff Tibballs

B☘XTREE

First published in
Great Britain in 1994 by
Boxtree Limited,
Broadwall House, 21 Broadwall, London SE1 9PL

Text © Geoff Tibballs 1993, 1994

10 8 6 4 2 1 3 5 7 9

A CIP catalogue entry for this book is available
from the British Library

ISBN 0 7522 0845 4

Front cover photograph by Pete Jones
Cover design by Martin Lovelock
Typeset by SX Composing Ltd, Rayleigh, Essex
Printed and bound in Great Britain by
BPC Paperbacks Ltd
A member of
The British Printing Company Ltd

CONTENTS

INTRODUCTION

The vast majority of us are fortunate enough to go through our lives without any connection with murder whatsoever . . . or so we think. I counted myself as one to whom the act of murder was just the yellowed pages of a book, a grainy newspaper photograph or the nightly images on the television news. But while researching *The Murder Guide to Great Britain*, I found that the school I attended in St Albans was perilously close to where the body of London gangster Red Max Kassel was dumped, that I bought our first car in the very street where the Luton Sack Murder was committed and that the publishers of this book are based just around the corner from where the infamous Dr Neill Cream claimed two of his victims. The moral is simple: the next time you buy a house, get a report of its history as well as a structural survey. Since this book is primarily concerned with murder sites, in a few of the more recent cases I have deliberately omitted the names of those concerned to avoid causing unnecessary distress to their families. I hope I have succeeded.

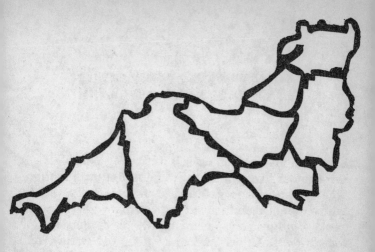

SOUTH-
WEST OF
ENGLAND

AVON

Bath: 'Wallasey', Englishcombe Lane

Vacuum cleaner salesman Reginald Hinks wanted Constance Pullen for one thing — her £2,000 inheritance. Divorcee Constance lived with her 85-year-old senile father James in a large house at 43 Milton Avenue, Bath. Then Hinks swept her off her feet and they married in March 1933, whereupon he immediately set about getting rid of the old man so that he could lay his hands on the money. Using £900 of his father-in-law's cash, Hinks moved the family to a smaller residence — 'Wallasey', a small villa in Englishcombe Lane. At first, he endeavoured to encourage the frail Mr Pullen to die naturally. He dismissed Mr Pullen's nurse and placed his would-be benefactor on a strict diet in the hope that he would fade away altogether. Next, Mr Pullen was subjected to a series of rigorous walks or sometimes merely left to wander outside alone in the cold. But Mr Pullen flatly refused to die and furthermore, his lawyer had barred Hinks' access to any more of the family money. So Hinks decided to take more drastic action. On 1 December 1933, he telephoned the Fire Brigade and told them that he had found Mr Pullen dead with his head in the oven. He explained: 'If you find a bruise on the back of his head, that happened when I pulled him out of the oven.' However, it was proved that the bruise had been caused before death and Reginald Hinks was hanged on 4 May 1934.

3

Bristol: College Green

Situated between the Cathedral and the Church of St Augustine, College Green was the setting for a particularly brutal murder on 28 September 1764 when Mrs Frances Ruscombe was butchered in her house along with her maid Mary Champneys. Mrs Ruscombe's body was found on the stairs near the front door. Her throat had been slit, one of her eyes had been beaten out and she had been battered so ferociously around the head with a hammer that pieces of her shattered skull had been driven into her brain. Mary Champneys' corpse lay in the back parlour. Her head was practically severed from her neck and her skull had been split in two by a weapon believed to have been an axe. Their killer was Edward Higgins, a hardened criminal, who carried out the heinous act in the course of a robbery. He remained at large for some time before being apprehended in the wake of a string of burglaries. Higgins was sentenced to death and finally confessed to the College Green murders on the eve of his execution in November 1767.

Bristol: Lloyds Bank, North View

Two young Poles, Roman Redel and Zbigniew Gower, were unemployed and desperately short of money. So when they spotted the small branch of Lloyds in North View from the top deck of a passing Corporation bus, they decided to rob it. They reckoned it was an easy target. They had intended stealing a motorbike for transport but got so drunk the night before the raid that they were incapable of riding it. Instead they travelled to the bank on the morning of Monday 13 March 1950 by bus. Inside the bank, Redel brandished a revolver while his accomplice vaulted the counter to collect the spoils. But Gower was nervously looking over his shoulder all the time and wasn't concentrating on what he was picking up. It was later calculated that he stole the princely sum of £28 plus a stack of worthless paying-in slips. With no getaway arranged, the pair jumped on another bus, only for the bank guard, whom they had not thought to tie up, to halt the driver with a cry of 'Stop! Bandits are on your bus!' The bungling duo fled on foot, pursued by a posse of passers-by, but here comedy turned to tragedy as Redel was overhauled by keep-fit fanatic Bob Taylor. A violent struggle ensued and Redel killed him with a gunshot to the head. Both Redel and Gower were hanged.

Bristol: Hill Avenue, Bedminster

Sixty-one-year-old widower Roy Page ran a corner tobacconist's and sweetshop in the Bedminster area of Bristol. He lived at the back of the premises and was a popular figure locally. But on 18 July 1985, he was found dead in his shop, having been savagely beaten about the head with a gag forced down his throat. All the gas appliances had been turned on and nearly £2,000 had been stolen. Mr Page had been killed around 6 pm, the victim of bogus gasman Clive Richards, a 34-year-old Welshman. Richards had been scouring Bristol that day, claiming to be looking for gas leaks, and had visited at least four other similar shops in the city. He was eventually caught after performing his bogus gasman routine in Portsmouth, apparently unaware that his 'act' had featured heavily on the BBC's *Crimewatch UK*. When approached by the police, Richards claimed to be a professor but was found in possession of an iron bar and a knife, not implements usually associated with a university don. He was subsequently sentenced to life imprisonment.

Horton: Widdenhill Farm

The sleepy village of Horton lies a couple of miles to the north-east of Chipping Sodbury and some ten miles from Bristol. But the rural tranquillity was shattered on 30 April 1984 when nearby Widdenhill Farm was the scene of a mysterious murder. Graham Backhouse, 44, was a struggling farmer, whose overdraft had risen to £70,000. He had claimed that he was the victim of a hate campaign: a sheep's head had been impaled on a fence at the farm with a note attached which read, 'You next' and then, on 9 April, his wife Margaret had miraculously survived an attempt to blow her up with a car bomb. Three weeks later, the police arrived at Widdenhill Farm to find Backhouse covered in blood while the dead body of a neighbour lay in the hall at the foot of the stairs. He had been shot. Backhouse insisted that the dead man had admitted planting the bomb and had attacked him with a Stanley knife whereupon Backhouse had seized a shotgun and fired in self-defence. But a quite different story began to emerge when it was learned that a month before the car bomb, Backhouse had increased his wife's life insurance from £50,000 to £100,000. When Backhouse's plot to kill her failed, he had lured the neighbour to the farm, shot him and deliberately slashed himself with the Stanley knife in the hope of throwing suspicion elsewhere. It also transpired that Backhouse had written the 'You next' note. He was given two terms of life imprisonment.

Winford

John Rogers, a 20-year-old brewery clerk, hatched a plan to rob a taxi driver. Accordingly, late on the evening of 29 July 1960, armed with a sawn-off shotgun, he got into the cab of driver William Tripp in Bristol city centre. As the taxi approached the village of Winford, some seven miles south of Bristol, Rogers told Mr Tripp to pull over but before the cab had stopped, Rogers shot the driver in the back of the head. The cab overturned in a hedge while Rogers took the money and fled, ending up at an August Bank Holiday jazz festival at Beaulieu in Hampshire. Rogers was soon arrested and found guilty of murder although he claimed his intention was only to rob. His death sentence was commuted to life imprisonment.

CORNWALL

Carrickowel, Porthpean

Overlooking picturesque St Austell Bay, Carrickowel provided the setting for one of the most infamous murders of 1952 – the slaying of his parents by 26-year-old Miles Giffard. Son of the Clerk to St Austell Magistrates, Giffard had always been the black sheep of the family. He was a wastrel and also a schizophrenic. He developed an infatuation for a 19-year-old girl named Gabrielle Vallance who lived in Chelsea but he was constantly frustrated by his father's refusal to allow him to travel up to London. Giffard's resentment reached the point where, in a letter to Gabrielle on 3 November, he wrote of his father: 'Short of doing him in, I see no future in the world at all.' Four days later, Giffard put that idea into practice. At 5.30 pm he phoned Gabrielle from Carrickowel to say that he might be coming up to London later that evening on business for his father, adding that he would call again at 8.30 pm to confirm. In the meantime, he was preoccupied with murdering his parents. At 7.30 he clubbed his father unconscious in the garage with a piece of iron piping. He then tracked down his mother in the kitchen and handed out similar treatment before returning to both parents and raining further blows on their heads. Once they were dead, Giffard loaded the bodies into a wheelbarrow and tipped them over the edge of the nearby cliff. Presumably to make it look like a robbery, he stole some of his dead mother's jewellery and having made the promised call to the unknowing Gabrielle, drove to London where he was arrested the following night. He had already pawned the jewellery. Giffard was duly found guilty of murder and executed.

Housel Bay Hotel, nr The Lizard

The summerhouse of the Housel Bay Hotel usually presented a peaceful haven from the atrocities of war but it was there that young soldier William Croft, a married man with two children, took the life of his lover Joan Lewis on 16 October 1943. Croft maintained that the two tormented souls had made a suicide pact fearing they were about to be parted. But neither appeared too keen to make the first move until, according to Croft, Joan placed a revolver next to her heart and pulled the trigger. However the shot wasn't sufficient to kill her and Croft claimed that it was when he went to fetch help, that he heard the fatal second shot. He said that he returned to find Joan lying on the floor, shot in the head. Croft stated that, in keeping with the pact, he then tried to shoot himself in the head but the gun wouldn't fire. However the pathologist revealed that Joan's wounds could not have been self-inflicted. As a result Croft was found guilty of murder and hanged.

Lewannick: Trenhorne House

Sarah Ann Hearn lived at Trenhorne House, Lewannick, four miles south-west of Launceston. Following the death of her invalid sister, Mrs Everard, in July 1930, Ann Hearn became friendly with next-door neighbours William and Alice Thomas of Trenhorne Farm and the trio used to set off together on day trips. One such expedition took them to the North Cornwall resort of Bude on 18 October 1930. At a café in the town they ordered food and also ate some salmon sandwiches prepared by Ann Hearn back at Trenhorne House. Later that day, Alice Thomas fell ill with suspected food poisoning, her condition deteriorating until she died on 4 November. The post-mortem revealed arsenic. Everyone's finger seemed to point at Ann Hearn with local gossip speculating that she wanted to marry William Thomas. She promptly disappeared after the funeral and faked her own suicide by leaving her coat on the cliffs at Looe. The police were not convinced and traced her to Torquay where she was working as a housekeeper using the poignant pseudonym, 'Mrs Faithful'. Ann Hearn was subsequently charged with the murders of both Mrs Thomas and Mrs Everard, the latter's body having been exhumed also to reveal traces of arsenic. But after an impassioned plea by her counsel, the estimable Mr Norman Birkett, Ann Hearn was found not guilty and walked free. The mystery of the Lewannick poisonings remains unsolved.

Titson, nr Marhamchurch

An isolated cottage in the hamlet of Titson near Marhamchurch, just south of Bude, was home to 84-year-old Richard Roadley. A local rumour had it that Mr Roadley had money hoarded away in the cottage which was music to the ears of rabbit trapper William Maynard. On 18 February 1928, 36-year-old Maynard broke into Roadley's house and struck the old man on the head, killing him. He then searched the house and stole any items of value before burying them on his father's farm nearby.

When questioned by the police, Maynard attempted to blame the murder on another man, Harris, who he claimed was his partner on the robbery. But Harris had an unbreakable alibi and Maynard was tried alone. Found guilty, Maynard was executed on 27 July 1928.

Tregonissey, nr St Austell

Insurance agent Edward Black was deeply in debt and deeply out of love with his wife Annie. She was 18 years older than him and ran a sweet shop in Tregonissey. Black decided to rid himself of her company and to this end bought two ounces of rat poison from Timothy White's store in St Austell and added it to her breakfast on 31 October 1921. She died on 11 November by which time Black had taken his leave of Cornwall and secreted himself in a temperance house in Liverpool. At first, the cause of death was given as gastro-enteritis from which Mrs Black was known to suffer but a post-mortem revealed arsenic poisoning. Black then tried to kill himself by slitting his throat but was caught and hung in Exeter on 24 March 1922.

DEVON

Babbacombe: 'The Glen'

Formerly a maid to Queen Victoria, Miss Emma Keyse had retired and lived comfortably at 'The Glen', a two-storey thatched cottage on the sea-front at Babbacombe in the heart of the bay. But although she was relatively wealthy, she didn't show much generosity to her staff, much to the annoyance of one of her footmen, 19-year-old John Lee. Matters came to a head when Miss Keyse reduced his already miserly wages as a result of a minor misdemeanour. Lee exacted a full and bloody revenge in the dining-room at 'The Glen' on 14 November 1884, battering his employer around the head and then slitting her throat. Leaving her dead on the floor, he proceeded to set fire to the room. Lee, who had previously served a prison sentence for theft, was found guilty of Miss Keyse's murder and sentenced to hang. But he became known as the man they could not hang, for three times he was placed on the hangman's trap and three times the trap refused to drop even though the mechanism was found to be in perfect working order. Consequently, his sentence was commuted to life imprisonment with Lee maintaining that, just before his day of reckoning, he had dreamed he would not hang. 'The Glen' has since been demolished and a hotel now stands on the site.

Thurlestone Sands

Situated some four miles west of Salcombe in South Devon, nowadays Thurlestone Sands is a popular beach with holidaymakers. But there wasn't much of a welcome from the locals in 1772 when strong winds forced the brig *Chanteloupe*, bound for Plymouth after setting out from the West Indies, to beach on Thurlestone Sands. Huge waves nearly capsized the ship and passengers were tossed into the sea where most swiftly perished. One hardy soul, Mrs Burke, managed to scramble ashore still wearing her most expensive jewellery and finest gown. Three men dragged her on to the sanctuary of the beach but far from being rescuers, they were callous robbers and murderers. They ripped off her earrings and, finding her rings too tight to remove, hacked off her fingers and stripped her of her clothing before burying her in the sand. Two weeks later, Daniel Whiddon, later immortalised in the song 'Uncle Tom Cobleigh', was walking his dog along the beach when it began digging in the sand and unearthed Mrs Burke's body. Her killers were never caught although it seems certain that some local villagers must have known their identity.

DORSET

Birdsmoorgate, nr Beaminster

Among the crowds gathered for the execution of Martha Brown at Dorchester on 9 August 1856 was a 16-year-old architect's apprentice named Thomas Hardy. The young man was so captivated by the experience that when he later turned his hand to writing novels, he partly based his heroine Tess of the d'Urbervilles on the hapless Martha. The act for which Martha paid the ultimate penalty was a true crime of passion. She was married to John Brown, a carrier, who was about 20 years her junior and had something of a roving eye. Rumour had it that he had only married Martha for her money. One day in 1856 Martha returned to their home in Birdsmoorgate to find him making love to another woman. That night a bitter argument developed during which John Brown hit his wife with his whip. She responded by felling him with an axe, killing him outright, and tried to pass off her husband's wounds by claiming that he had been kicked by his horse. But it was to no avail and Martha was set to enter folklore.

Bournemouth: Villa Madeira, Manor Road

Alma Rattenbury was a talented musician trapped in a loveless marriage with architect husband Francis who was 36 years older than her. Six years after their wedding, the vivacious Alma began an affair with George

Stoner, the Rattenburys' young chauffeur-cum-handyman, who was given a live-in position at their home, the Villa Madeira. On the night of 25 March 1935, Francis Rattenbury was beaten over the head with a mallet as he sat in his chair by the drawing-room fire and later died in hospital from a fractured skull. The lovers shielded each other by both confessing to the murder. Stoner maintained that he had struck out in a drug-inspired jealous rage. Ultimately, Alma was acquitted but Stoner was sentenced to die. Her life in ruins, Alma stabbed herself to death three days later by the river near Christchurch, upon which Stoner's sentence was commuted to life imprisonment. Nearly 60 years on, the case is still spoken of and the Villa Madeira still stands in its quiet side-road on the cliff above Bournemouth beach, a picnic setting for a notorious act of murder.

Bournemouth: Poole Road, Branksome

Widower Walter Dinivan, a wealthy retired garage owner, lived with his granddaughter in the ground floor flat of a large converted villa in Poole Road. The house was screened from the main road by a barrier of trees and shrubs and so there were no witnesses when Dinivan was violently attacked on 21 May 1939. He suffered ten wounds to the head and an attempt had been made to strangle him. He died the following morning. Money and jewellery were missing from the safe in the drawing-room but there was no sign of a break-in so the police suspected that Dinivan knew his killer. They arrested 69-year-old Joseph Williams, a friend of the deceased. Williams had fallen on hard times and was desperate for money. The case against him was overwhelming yet, incredibly, he was acquitted, only to confess to the murder a few hours later to a Fleet Street crime reporter, knowing that he couldn't be tried again on the same charge. Williams died in March 1951 and the following Sunday the *News of the World* duly printed their exclusive.

Bournemouth: Branksome Dene Chine

To the western end of Bournemouth promenade lies Branksome Dene Chine, a densely wooded area of great natural beauty leading from the affluent Branksome Park district down to the beach. It was here on 8 July 1946, in a secluded part of the chine, that the naked and mutilated body of Doreen Marshall was found dumped in rhododendron bushes. Her throat had been cut and a nipple had been bitten off after death. The 21-year-old former Wren was the victim of sadistic killer Neville Heath. On the run from murdering film extra Margery Gardner at a Notting Hill Gate hotel, Heath had arrived in Bournemouth and had booked into room 81 at the Tollard Royal Hotel on the West Cliff using the alias Group Captain Brooke. He quickly befriended Doreen Marshall who was staying at the Norfolk Hotel on Richmond Hill and they dined together at the Tollard Royal on the evening of 3 July. Shortly after midnight, Miss Marshall asked the porter for a taxi but Heath insisted on walking her back to her hotel. After killing her purely to satisfy his lust, Heath furtively climbed a ladder to re-enter his hotel room through the window. But incriminating evidence was discovered in Heath's belongings at Bournemouth West station and he was charged with murder. Despite pleading insanity, the 28-year-old RAF officer was hanged in October 1946.

Gussage St Michael: Sovel Plantation

Walter Burton worked as a rabbit catcher at Manor Farm, Gussage St Michael, and lived above the village post office with his schoolteacher wife and child. Mrs Burton was considerably older than her husband who enjoyed chasing younger women, notably 24-year-old Winifred Mitchell who was a cook at the farm. They began an affair with the prospect of emigrating to Canada but it all turned sour when he suspected she was pregnant. So instead of starting a new life with her, Burton decided to end hers altogether. On 29 March 1913, pretending to elope, he lured Winifred to the remote Sovel Plantation where he shot her with a borrowed gun. Her body was discovered over a month later in a shallow grave. Burton's fate was sealed by torn letters written by him and found at the farm. He was hanged at Dorchester Prison.

Sherborne: Coombe Farm Cottage

In 1935, squalid Coombe Farm Cottage was home to 33-year-old Charlotte Bryant, an illiterate mother of five, and her husband Frederick, a humble labourer. Charlotte was virtually toothless and her hair was infested with lice yet men seemed to find her irresistible and her reputation went before her in the inns of North Dorset. She became besotted with gypsy Leonard Parsons, who lodged at Coombe Farm, and decided to rid herself of her husband. So she slipped weed-killer in poor Fred's Oxo drink and on 22 December 1935, he died of poisoning. It was exactly the Christmas present Charlotte Bryant wanted. Less welcome was the noose round her neck at Exeter on 15 July 1936 after she was found guilty of murder.

GLOUCESTERSHIRE

Coleford: Fetterhill Farm

Harry Pace was a bully with a particular penchant for
beating his long-suffering wife Beatrice. In the summer
of 1927, he had been taken ill while dipping sheep at his
farm on the edge of the Forest of Dean and finally on 10
January 1928, he died. Harry's brother Elton was suspicious and claimed that he had once heard Beatrice
wishing 'the old bastard' was dead. A post-mortem was
ordered and arsenic was found in the body of the
deceased. Sheep dip contains arsenic but the 9.42 grains
found in Harry's body was deemed too great for natural
absorption through the skin. The Coroner's jury decreed
that Harry Pace had been poisoned and when pressed to
name the culprit, they suggested Beatrice Pace. At
Beatrice's trial, the defence claimed that the death was
suicide. Ultimately the judge decided there was insufficient evidence to continue, and so instructed the jury to
return a formal verdict of not guilty. Beatrice Pace
walked free – from the law and her husband. But the
mystery of Harry's death remains.

Lydney: Purlieu End Bungalow

On 28 June 1964, two boys were scouring Bracknell
Woods in Berkshire, not far from Blackhill Road, in
search of bait for a fishing expedition. A few feet off a
forest path on a pile of rough turf, the delighted boys

stumbled across a mass of wriggling white maggots. As they pulled the turfs away to unearth the source of their riches, their joy turned to horror as in the midst of the insects lay a decomposed human forearm. It belonged to 42-year-old Peter Thomas who had been missing from his ramshackle wooden bungalow three miles outside Lydney since 16 or 17 June. It emerged that he had lent William Brittle, a heating engineer salesman from Hook in Hampshire, £2,000 and that the loan was due to be repaid that June. Brittle stated that he had returned the money to Thomas on the day he disappeared following a win on the horses but was unable to remember the names of any of the beasts which had earned him such a substantial windfall. He was found guilty of murder and sentenced to life imprisonment, the belief being that Thomas had been killed by a karate chop at his bungalow and then been driven to Bracknell in the boot of Brittle's car.

Gloucester: 25 Cromwell Street

Christened the 'House of Horror', this modest three-storey Victorian semi, nestling in a quiet street in the shadow of Gloucester Cathedral, has taken over from 195 Melrose Avenue and 10 Rillington Place as Britain's most notorious address. It first hit the headlines in February 1994 when police, acting on a tip-off, began digging in the home and garden of a 52-year-old builder Fred West. Four months later, they completed the search, having unearthed the remains of nine bodies. In the course of the extensive operation, police used seismic radar equipment to 'see through' walls and floors and a JCB to dig up the back garden. The first skeleton to be found was that of West's 16-year-old daughter

Heather who had vanished suddenly in May 1987. Three of the bodies were found beneath a large garden patio, laid by West in the summer of 1987, and partially screened from the outside world by a row of tall cypress trees. At around the same time, the cellar floor had been re-concreted. Five sets of human remains were discovered there, under the 6ft layer of concrete. The other body was found beneath the bathroom floor. In addition, the remains of West's eight-year-old daughter Charmaine, who had disappeared in 1972, were found beneath the kitchen floor of his former home, 25 Midland Road, Gloucester, (less than half a mile away from Cromwell Street) and two more bodies, including that of his first wife, Catherine Costello, were unearthed from Fingerpost Field near the Hereford and Worcester village of Much Marcle where West grew up. Twenty-five Cromwell Street, with its grubby net curtains and lime green window frames, had been extensively added to by West who had lived there with his second wife Rosemary for over 20 years. Stunned neighbours described them as 'perfectly normal'. One said, 'I used to see him go off to work and he would always wave a cheery hello.' At the time of writing, West had been charged with the murders of 11 young women, nine of them jointly with 40-year-old Rosemary.

SOMERSET

Great Wood Forest nr Over Stowey

On 4 April 1988, the badly decomposed body of a woman was found floating in a brook in Great Wood Forest in the heart of Somerset's Quantock Hills. She had been battered to death with a heavy rock. The woman, who had only been married for four weeks, had disappeared in October 1987 after a late-evening shopping trip in her home city of Bristol. She was last seen alive at around 8pm as she left Debenhams department store. Her orange Mini Clubman Estate was later found in a lock-up garage rented by 33-year-old John Cannan at Leigh Woods, Bristol. It emerged that the day before kidnapping his victim, Cannan had unsuccessfully tried to abduct a business-woman at gunpoint from a Bristol car park. A female witness at the murder trial spoke of hearing screams coming from the direction of trees near Cannan's luxury apartment in Leigh Woods on the afternoon of 9 October 1987. She also said she saw a man beating something with his hands. Cannan was found guilty of murder and jailed for life.

Kingsbury Episcopi

It seems inconceivable that a village with such a delightful name as Kingsbury Episcopi should ever have been host to cold-blooded murder. Yet on the night of 25

August 1956 this beautiful spot, eight miles west of Yeovil, witnessed the final act in the troubled marriage of Freda and Albert Rumbold. A timber contractor by trade, Albert was an odd character, given to behaving in a particularly bizarre manner whenever there was a full moon. It appears that Freda finally decided she could take no more and on the fateful night, she entered her husband's bedroom while he lay asleep and shot him in the head with his own shotgun. She attempted to cover up the crime by thrusting a towel soaked with perfume under Albert's bedroom door to camouflage the stench of decomposing flesh and hung a notice on the door saying 'PLEASE DO NOT ENTER'. But Albert's relatives were suspicious about his disappearance and the police soon found the body. Freda vowed that the gun had gone off accidentally during a quarrel but the manner in which the bullets had entered the deceased revealed her lie. She was sentenced to life imprisonment.

Wembdon, nr Bridgwater

When 26-year-old Lily Palmer found herself seated next to young labourer Ronald Atwell at the cinema, she agreed to go out for a drink with him one night. On 14 April 1950 Lily, who was mentally retarded, went with Atwell to the Horse and Jockey in Bridgewater where a local farmer, Davey, saw them leave shortly after 9.30 pm. Davey was the last witness to see Lily alive and by a macabre coincidence the first to see her dead. For the following morning he was walking from his house at Wembdon, just west of Bridgwater, to the farm outbuildings when he noticed some clothing fluttering in the hedge in a nearby field. On further investigation, he discovered Lily's battered body, naked apart from her stockings and shoes. Atwell, who had punched, kicked and strangled Lily in a fit of temper, claimed he was annoyed because Lily had said she had been with another man a few hours earlier. Atwell was hanged on 13 July 1950.

Wheal Eliza Mine, nr Simonsbath

William Burgess lived in a cottage at White Water on Exmoor but following the death of his wife, he went into lodgings at Gallon House Cot in Simonsbath, taking with him the youngest of his three children, seven-year-old Anna. One Sunday in June 1858, Burgess left his lodgings, telling the landlady that he was taking Anna to stay with her grandmother at Porlock Weir. Instead he killed his daughter and buried her in a tiny grave on the moor about a mile from Gallon House Inn. However, as he was crossing the moor some time after the murder, Burgess spotted two men examining the disturbed earth in search of a sheep. So he hastily moved the body. But Burgess had little hope of avoiding detection and was hanged at Taunton on 4 January 1859. At the trial it transpired that Burgess had killed little Anna so that he could spend the half crown a week it cost to keep her in lodgings on his own ale consumption.

Woodford

5 July 1773 was a warm summer's day in the hamlet of Woodford, a mile north of Monksilver on the Wiveliscombe-Watchet road. It was so serene that Elizabeth Conibeer, aged 88, and her two daughters, Anne, 45, and Sarah, 43, who lived in a quaint cottage in Woodford, left the front door open while they ate dinner in the

kitchen. This was also partly in anticipation of the regular visit from the baker's boy for whom they had left a small pile of pennies on the table. Suddenly the tranquillity was shattered when an unknown attacker burst in and stabbed all three women to death in a horrific orgy of violence. They didn't even have time to scream, for the baker's boy was a mere 100 yards away and heard nothing. When he called at the cottage shortly afterwards, the front door was half open. He took one look at the gruesome sight in the kitchen and raced off to raise the alarm. There was no motive and nobody was ever charged with the butchery at Woodford.

WILTSHIRE

Nr Netheravon

Sergeant William Crouch and PC Ernest Pike were colleagues in the Wiltshire Constabulary back in 1913. Crouch was stationed at Netheravon while Pike was the village constable at nearby Enford. Pike had a history of drink-related problems which had seen him regularly transferred but he became distraught when Sergeant Crouch accused him of being in the Three Horseshoes public house at Enford while on duty. In March 1913, PC Pike had an 11 pm meeting with Sergeant Crouch at a lonely spot on the Enford-Netheravon road, close to where a foot-path led off to Fittleton. The next morning under a clump of trees near the footpath, the body of Sergeant Crouch was found. The top of his head had been blown off by a shotgun. A few hundred yards downstream lay the body of PC Pike. He had shot himself in the head. Perhaps he hadn't been able to bear the thought of yet another transfer.

Warminster Barracks

One night in January 1918, a shot rang out in the barracks of the Canadian Corps, stationed at Warminster. A Corporal Dunkin was found sprawled on the bed. On the floor lay a .303 Lee-Enfield rifle with the breech open. The bullet had entered Dunkin at the left temple and exited just behind his right ear, passing through his pillow, kitbag and the hut wall before lodging in the ground outside. It suggested suicide but experts pointed out that the arms of the deceased were not long enough to have killed himself in such a position. The killer turned out to be a Private Asser who had harboured a deep-rooted grudge against the Corporal.

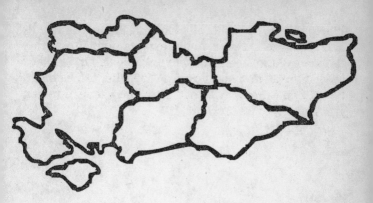

SOUTH
OF
ENGLAND

BERKSHIRE

Clewes: Arthur Road

Charles Woolridge, a 30-year-old trooper in the Royal Horse Guards, was living in barracks at Regent's Park, London, while his newly-married wife Ellen stayed at home alone in the village of Clewes near Windsor. She resided at 21 Alma Terrace on Arthur Road, a thoroughfare which led from Windsor Great Western station to Clewes village. Their enforced separation began to place a strain on the relationship even to the point that Ellen re-adopted her maiden name. She even presented her husband with a document to sign declaring that he would not molest her. When, on 29 March 1896, she failed to meet him at the barracks as arranged, he marched out of his quarters and headed for Windsor. That evening, Ellen's neighbours heard violent screams and saw Woolridge in the street standing over his wife's body. He had slit her throat. Found guilty of murder, Charles Woolridge was hung at Reading on 7 July 1896, but his memory was later immortalised in Oscar Wilde's dedication to *The Ballad of Reading Gaol*.

Hungerford

This peaceful town on the Berkshire Downs achieved worldwide notoriety when Michael Ryan shot 16 people dead and wounded 14 others in what became known as The Hungerford Massacre. 19 August 1987 started just like any other day until just before lunch when 27-year-old Ryan, dressed in combat gear and heavily armed, encountered a young mother walking with her two children in Savernake Forest. As the woman tried to escape, Ryan mercilessly cut her down with a burst of fire. Ten minutes later, he drove into Hungerford and calmly walked into the small house in South View where he lived with his mother. He shot his mother and the family dog and then proceeded to run amok in the town with his Kalashnikov semi-automatic assault rifle, indiscriminately mowing down anyone who was unfortunate enough to cross his path. Ryan then holed up in the John O'Gaunt School, which he had attended as a boy, before finally shooting himself in the head around 6 pm. The reign of terror was over but the citizens of Hungerford will never forget.

Maidenhead: Wynford, Ray Park Avenue

Wynford was the 17-room house of 94-year-old Mrs Freeman Lee who lived alone as a recluse. She had no money although local rumour suggested otherwise. On 1 June 1948, her milkman noticed that her bottles had been left on the step for two days and alerted the police. They found her body doubled up in a trunk in the hall. She had been battered, tied up and had slowly suffocated to death, probably in the trunk. The house was in an appalling stage of neglect (she had only actually lived in one room) but finger-prints on the lid of a small box led police to small-time housebreaker George Russell. He was traced to a tramps' hostel in St Albans and admitted having been at Wynford but said that Mrs Lee had employed him to do some gardening. However, the evidence against Russell was such that he was found guilty and hanged at Oxford on 2 December 1948.

Reading: Piggott's Road, Lower Caversham

Short and squat with her white hair tied rigidly in a bun, Bristol-born Amelia Dyer, a former member of the Salvation Army, became infamous as the Reading Baby Farmer. She moved around the country in Victorian times, using different names, offering to provide board for children. Once she had charge of them, she quickly killed the children but continued to draw the boarding fees. Under the guise of Mrs Thomas, she plied her evil trade in Caversham, then a village just outside Reading, first from Piggott's Road and later from Kensington Road. On 30 March 1896, a bargeman on the Thames at Reading fished the body of 15-month-old girl out of the river. It had been wrapped in a brown paper parcel and weighted with a brick. The infant had been strangled with a tape. On the paper was inscribed 'Mrs Thomas, Piggott's Road, Lower Caversham'. Dyer moved on but was arrested following further child murders. She killed seven in all, coldly commenting: 'You'll know all mine by the tape round their necks.' At the age of 57, Amelia Dyer was hanged at Newgate on 10 June 1896. She had lived considerably longer than those who were placed in her care.

Slough: Bath Place, Salt Hill

John Tawell was a Quaker, well respected throughout Berkshire for his charitable deeds. A chemist by profession, he gave the impression of being extremely wealthy but behind the glossy veneer lay quite a different story. For this pious pillar of society was not only a retired forger, who had previously missed the death penalty by the merest whisker, but he also kept a secret mistress, Sarah Hart. Nor was he rich – in fact he was so impoverished that he could no longer afford to keep paying Sarah her allowance of £1 a week. So he decided to murder her. After an unsuccessful attempt to poison his mistress's favourite stout tipple two years earlier, Tawell made the deed his New Year's resolution for 1845. On the morning of 1 January, he bought a quantity of prussic acid from a chemist in London's Bishopsgate and headed for Sarah's home at Bath Place in Slough. Once there, he sent her out to fetch some stout. Between 6 and 7 pm, a neighbour heard stifled screams and saw Tawell leaving the cottage. Sarah was found writing on the floor, dying a few minutes later. This time there was no escape for John Tawell and he was hanged on 28 March.

Slough: 22 High Street

Back in 1910, 22 High Street was the site of a small second-hand clothes shop run by an elderly lady named Mrs Wilson. On Friday 15 July that year, she was found dead in her shop. She had been badly beaten, her hands were tied across her chest and a cushion was tied over her face, causing death by suffocation. Her killer was car mechanic William Broome whose father owned the shop next door. Broome claimed he was in London on the day of the murder, applying for a job as a taxi driver, but a search of his room near Regent's Park revealed an envelope containing £20 in gold coins which had been stolen from Mrs Wilson. Scratches on his face resulting from his struggle with the old woman provided further evidence. Broome was found guilty of murder and executed.

CHANNEL ISLANDS

Guernsey: Bon Port Hotel, St Martin

The night of Sunday 1 October 1972 marked the end-of-season party for the 13 employees of the cliffside Bon Port Hotel at St Martin. With no guests to be served breakfast the following morning, the party went on well into the night, ending at around 1.30 am. The staff slowly retired, leaving just the kitchen porter, 21-year-old John Tilley from Taplow, Buckinghamshire, and 34-year-old chambermaid Margaret Weaver talking in the kitchen. The following morning there was no sign of Miss Weaver and it was not until Tuesday 3 October that her body was found buried in a shallow grave in a field 50 yards from the kitchen. She had died from multiple head injuries. It emerged that Tilley had killed Miss Weaver, described as something of a loner, after she had gone to his room and been highly critical of his girlfriend who also worked at the hotel. Tilley hit her repeatedly and kicked her in the face. After digging a hole and burying her, he went for a walk on his own. Tilley was found guilty of murder and sentenced to life imprisonment.

Guernsey: Les Pins nr St Peter Port

Until 30 June 1947, 53-year-old gardener James Ozanne had led a blameless life. His wife had died during the German occupation and he had looked after his two children single-handedly. But it had been a constant

33

struggle to feed them and make ends meet. Help was at hand in 1945 when, at the end of the German occupation, 40-year-old widow Clara Ogier went to work as housekeeper for Ozanne at his home, Les Pins. Then two years later came a massive bodyblow. Clara told Ozanne that she would soon be leaving his employment to get married. She handed in her notice on 30 June but shortly before 5 pm, Ozanne shot her in the head with a rifle as she brought in the washing. He then covered the body with a sack before catching a bus to St Peter Port police station to report his crime. The thought of once again being left alone to raise his family had been too much for him. He was found guilty but the death sentence was commuted.

Jersey: Mont a la Brune, St Brelades

Saturday 4 April 1959 was a perfect day for a picnic and so the Heath family filled their hamper and set off for the dunes near Mont a la Brune. The two children happily dug in the sand – until they uncovered the black toe-cap of a man's shoe. Their mother took over and scraped back the sand to reveal the body of 45-year-old John Perree. He had been shot in the face while urinating. That much was evident from the fact that his fly was open and his left hand was partly in his trouser pocket. The dead man's glass eye lay on the ground some six feet away. Perree, a drain-layer who was unmarried and lived with his sister and brother-in-law at Mont Les Vaux, had been murdered on Easter Monday. He had been drinking that night at the Horse and Hound in St Brelade with 32-year-old Francis Huchet. Spotting Perree's wad of five-pound notes, Huchet had shot him in the dunes at a vulnerable moment. Huchet then covered the body with sand but when he tried to drive his car away, it stuck in the sand and he had to borrow a lorry to tow the vehicle clear. When charged, Huchet attempted to save his neck by writing an anonymous letter, blaming two fictitious men. It was an act of supreme folly and Huchet was found guilty of murder and hanged.

Jersey: St Brelades, Close de l'Atlantique

One of Jersey's biggest mysteries was sparked on 10 October 1987 by the disappearance of 57-year-old Lloyd's underwriter Nicholas Newall and his wife Elizabeth from their £200,000 bungalow at St Brelades. They had last been seen alive in the restaurant of the Sea Crest Hotel, St Brelades, celebrating Mrs Newall's 48th birthday. Traces of blood were found at the bungalow but there was no sign of any bodies. Rumour was rife throughout the island, much of it surrounding the Newalls' eldest son Roderick, a lieutenant with the Royal Green Jackets regiment. It was further fuelled in 1991 when he and his brother Mark, a money broker, inherited an estimated £400,000 after winning an application at Jersey's Royal Court in St Helier to have their parents presumed dead. The police never gave up. Five years after the disappearance, they secretly recorded a meeting between Roderick and an uncle, the spitting image of Nicholas Newall, at a hotel in Perthshire. Gazing into the face of his dead father's identical twin, Roderick Newall blurted out his pent-up guilt and was later arrested at sea, 150 miles off Gibraltar, in August 1993. After being extradited to the UK, 28-year-old Roderick confessed to the murders and told the police where his parents' bodies were buried. Wrapped in black plastic, they were exhumed from a 3 ft grave in a wooded valley at Greve de Lecq on the north of the island. Committal proceedings heard that both brothers had attended the champagne celebration dinner but Mark left after the meal. Back at the bungalow a heated argument broke out between Roderick and his father, in which a lot of old wounds were reopened. As the drunken row escalated, it is alleged that Roderick killed his parents with a martial arts rice flail, his father in the sitting room, his mother in the master bedroom. He then phoned Mark, vowing to kill himself. To stop Roderick committing suicide, Mark helped to bury the bodies. Seven years on, it seems that the mystery of St Brelades has finally been solved.

EAST SUSSEX

Brighton: Gloucester Place

Spinster Christiana Edmunds was 43 and lived with her widowed mother in a splendid house in Gloucester Place facing St Peter's Church. She became besotted with married physician Dr Beard and in March 1871 called at the doctor's house with a box of sweets. Alone with Mrs Beard, Edmunds offered her a chocolate cream which immediately made the doctor's wife severely ill. As a result, Dr Beard accused Edmunds of trying to poison his wife. Incensed by the charge, Edmunds manically set about proving that there was a poisoner at large in Brighton. During her gentle afternoon walks, she would bribe children into buying chocolate creams from a particular sweet shop. She would then take the sweets home and in the privacy of her bedroom, inject them with strychnine before carefully re-wrapping them. She would then persuade another boy to exchange them at the same shop for smaller ones, thus leaving the innocent shop-keeper to sell her poisoned sweets. After one such sortie, four-year-old Sidney Barker died within 20 minutes of eating a sweet from a bag bought by his uncle. Edmunds progressed to cakes and fruit sent through the post, even addressing some to herself to underline her innocence, and criticised the police for not apprehending the poisoner who was terrifying the town. Finally, she was caught and sent to Broadmoor where she died in 1907.

Brighton Railway Station

In the summer of 1934, Brighton made international headlines as the police found themselves simultaneously investigating two trunk murders. At the height of rush-hour on Derby Day, 6 June, a trunk had been deposited in the left-luggage office at the station. Eleven days later, an attendant appalled by the awful stench wafting from within, summoned the police to force the locks and inside they discovered a woman's torso wrapped in brown paper. The head and limbs were missing although the legs were found in a suitcase deposited in the left-luggage office at King's Cross station the next day. Despite extensive inquiries spanning four countries, neither the victim nor the killer were ever identified.

Brighton: 44 Park Crescent

While probing the above case, the police stumbled across another woman's body in a trunk, barely 200 yards from the station, at 52 Kemp Street. The victim was 42-year-old Violette Kaye (real name Violet Saunders), a blonde ex-showgirl who had turned to prostitution. She and her boyfriend, small-time crook Tony Mancini, lived in a basement at 44 Park Crescent while Macini took a waitering job at the Skylark Café on the sea-front. On 10 May 1934, after the two had argued at the café, Violette disappeared. Mancini told friends that she had gone to Paris but the truth was that she was dead, felled by a series of blows to the head. Mancini then moved to a basement flat at 52 Kemp Street where he kept Violette's corpse in a trunk for two months. The malodour worsened to the point that visitors asked him whether he kept rabbits. On 15 July, police investigating the station trunk murder, heard about Violette's disappearance and found her decomposing body at Kemp Street. Mancini was the obvious suspect but at his trial he insisted that Violette was already dead on the bed at 44 Park Crescent when he had returned home from work. He was found not guilty but in 1976, under a story headlined I'VE GOT AWAY WITH MURDER, Mancini told the *News of the World* that he had been responsible for Violette's death after all.

Crowborough: Wesley Poultry Farm, Blackness

Norman Thorne, a 24-year-old chicken farmer and Sunday school teacher, lived in a ramshackle hut on his small-holding at Crowborough which he called the Wesley Poultry Farm. He was engaged to Elsie Cameron, a rather plain London typist, who was so desperate for marriage that she pretended she was pregnant. Meanwhile Thorne had met a fun-loving local dressmaker, Bessie Caldicott, who he considered to be much better company than the neurotic Elsie. So he wrote to Elsie telling her about his new love. Elsie was furious and on 5 December 1924, she arrived in Crowborough, but was never to be seen in one piece again. For at the farm Thorne dissected her with a hacksaw. He put her head in a biscuit tin, wrapped her limbs in newspapers and buried her under the chicken-run where he kept his Leghorns. He even had the nerve to pose for press photographers, covering Elsie's disappearance, on the actual spot beneath which he had buried her body. Thorne eventually admitted chopping up Elsie's body but maintained that he had found her hanging from a beam in the hut. The means by which she died was never truly established but Norman Thorne was found guilty of murder and hanged.

The Crumbles

A desolate area of shingle beach stretching from Eastbourne to Pevensey Bay and known as the Crumbles witnessed two particularly unpleasant murders of young women in the early 1920s. In the summer of 1920, Irene Munro, an attractive 17-year-old typist from London, was holidaying alone in Eastbourne. During her first week there, on the afternoon of 19 August, Irene left her guest house and was seen walking with two men in the direction of the Crumbles. Her fully-clothed body was later found partially buried in the shingle, 500 yards from a disused railway carriage. Her straw hat was pulled over her battered face and weighted down by stones. Witnesses identified the men as two unemployed locals, Jack Field and William Gray. Field had previous convictions for robbery and Gray, who was illiterate, had once raped a girl. It is believed that Irene was killed for spurning their sexual advances. Field and Gray were hanged on 4 February 1921.

The Crumbles: The Officer's House, nr Langney

Four years after the murder of Irene Munro, the Crumbles was in the news again when another typist, 37-year-old Emily Kaye, was butchered in a bungalow known as the Officer's House which had once been the home of the local coastguard officer. Miss Kaye had become infatuated with handsome Patrick Mahon, a dapper criminal with a weakness for women. Although he was married, he had made Emily pregnant and was slowly fleecing her of her savings. On 12 April 1924, Mahon bought a cook's knife and a saw before travelling down to the Officer's House which he had rented under the name of Waller. There he awaited the arrival of Emily who had been lured to the coast by the prospect of living together with her loved one. But when Mahon began to renege on some of his promises, there was a fearful argument and he killed her with a blow to the head from an axe. Next he set about cutting up the body, severing the head before burning it in the sitting-room grate along with the feet and legs. He then invited another young woman, Miss Ethel Duncan, to spend Easter with him at the bungalow and they shared a bedroom while Miss Kaye's dismembered body lay rotting in a trunk in an adjoining room. Mahon later boiled other bodily portions in a large pot, discarding them from a train somewhere between Waterloo and Reading. When Mahon's suspicious wife led police to her husband and the bungalow was searched, local residents flocked to peer over the garden fence to watch the grisly remains being brought out. At his trial, Mahon stated that Emily had died after banging her head on a coal scuttle but nevertheless he was found guilty and hanged for what the Director of Public Prosecutions described as 'one of the foulest crimes which has been committed in recent years.'

HAMPSHIRE

Aldershot: Long Valley

A bizarre game that went wrong resulted in the discovery of the body of 21-year-old James Ellis, a drummer in the Leicestershire Regiment, on 26 September 1923. His remains, little more than a skeleton, were found under bushes in Long Valley on the edge of Aldershot. He had been dead for four months, having suffocated while tied up and gagged, his face covered with a military great-coat, held in place by a belt fastened around his head. He had been killed by his friend, Lance-Corporal Albert Dearnley. On the evening of 24 May, Dearnley and Ellis had gone for a walk on a common near their barracks in Aldershot and had played a game using a drum-rope as a lasso. Dearnley then tied Ellis up at his own request but left him bound and gagged in the bushes as punishment for having insulted Dearnley's girlfriend. Dearnley hadn't intended killing Ellis and said that he had meant to release him the next morning but had overslept. He then assumed Ellis had managed to free himself and had simply deserted. Even so, Dearnley was sentenced to death. His coffin was prepared but he was reprieved at the last minute.

Alton: The Hollow

When she set out to play with friends on a balmy summer Saturday in 1867, seven-year-old Fanny Adams knew nothing of the fate that was soon to befall her nor of the legend that would arise from her death. On 24 August, Fanny and her little sister Lizzie left their home in Tan House Lane, Alton, to play with their friend Minnie Warner half a mile away in Flood Meadow near the River Wey on the outskirts of town. There they met friendly local solicitor Frederick Baker who offered the girls ha'pennies if they would go with him to The Hollow, a quiet country road leading to Shalden village. They agreed but when he asked Fanny to come alone with him into a hop plantation at the top of The Hollow, they had their doubts. Baker removed their anxiety by giving Minnie and Lizzie another ha'penny each and told them to run home while he playfully picked Fanny up and carried her into the hops. When Fanny didn't return, a search was launched and her horrifically mutilated body was found in the plantation. She had been battered to death. Her head was stuck on a hop-pole, her eyes gouged out. The eyes were later found in the river and other portions of her body were located nearby. Baker was arrested and in his diary was the damning entry: 'Saturday August 24th. Killed a young girl. It was fine and hot.' Baker was duly hanged but the term 'Sweet Fanny Adams' was born. It came about when tinned rations were introduced in the navy. None of the sailors knew what they were eating from the tin and one jokingly suggested the meat was Sweet Fanny Adams.

Bignell Wood, nr Cadnam

Albert Goozee, a 32-year-old fitter's mate, had been a lodger with Tom Leakey and his wife Lydia at their home in Parkstone, Bournemouth. It had been a curious set-up for Goozee was not only having an affair with 53-year-old Mrs Leakey but had also shown an unhealthy interest in her 14-year-old daughter Norma. Goozee then moved out but was still not free of Mrs Leakey who not only wanted to continue the affair but, according to Goozee, was threatening to expose his inclinations towards Norma. On 17 June 1956, this *ménage à trois* set out for a picnic to Bignell Wood on the fringes of the New Forest, about six miles west of Southampton. They pitched camp by a track leading to Canterton Glen and in this idyllic setting Goozee decided to butcher the two objects of his infatuation. The two bodies of Mrs Leakey and Norma were later found next to the dying embers of the picnic fire. They had been stabbed to death and Goozee had also attacked Mrs Leakey with an axe. To shift the blame, Goozee stabbed himself, claiming that the women had gone mad and had started attacking each other and him. But Goozee was found guilty of murder and sentenced to life imprisonment. It is interesting to note that at the time of the murder Goozee was working at the Tollard Royal Hotel, Bournemouth, where evil Neville Heath had stayed.

Bordon Camp

A hut on the edge of Bordon Camp, some seven miles south of Farnham, served as a bank on certain days of the week, a temptation which proved too great for 18-year-old Lance-Corporal Jack Goldenberg of the East Lancashire Regiment. Thursday was pay-day for the 6,000 or so troops stationed at the camp and early one afternoon in April 1924, Goldenberg walked in to the hut and told the bank manager William Hall to raise his hands. The plucky manager made a dive for the drawer beneath the counter where he kept his gun but before he could reach it, Goldenberg shot him three times with a revolver. The murderer tried to throw the police off the scent by helpfully informing them that he had seen two civilians acting suspiciously in a car parked close to the bank but his fate was sealed when a warrant officer spotted him furtively entering a locked hut. Hidden inside the hut was £500 of the stolen money. Goldenberg confessed to the crime and was later hanged.

Fordingbridge: Burgate House

Standing at the end of a long drive, shared only with the headquarters of the Game Conservancy, imposing Burgate House was home to a wealthy retired publisher, his invalid wife and her nurse. Also staying there on the night of 31 August 1986 were the youngest of the couple's three sons and his wife. During dinner, a three-man gang burst in brandishing guns seized from a cupboard in the hall. The family were forced upstairs where the daughter-in-law was brutally raped and strangled. The others were tied up, doused with petrol and set ablaze with firelighters, burning to death in excruciating pain. The son, who had lost a leg in a car accident, struggled free by slipping off his artificial leg but perished trying to reach the safety of a window. The gang had hoped that the fire would destroy all evidence of the five murders but the house was built largely from concrete and so little structural damage was done. The trail quickly led to George Stephenson, 36, who had been dismissed as handyman at Burgate House six weeks previously. He had recruited brothers John and George Daly, telling them the house was full of valuables and the guns they needed for a future armed robbery. But what Stephenson really wanted was a murderous revenge for his sacking – and so he took along firelighters and petrol. Stephenson was convicted of four murders and given six life sentences with the recommendation that he serve at least 25 years; John Daly, found guilty of all five murders, rape and robbery, received seven life sentences; and George Daly got 24 years for rape, robbery and four charges of manslaughter. As for Burgate House, it was put on the market but not surprisingly there were no buyers. So the House of Horrors, as it had become known, was bulldozed and the land sold for £600,000.

Portsmouth: Baffins Farm, Copnor

The coachman to a respectable Teignmouth doctor, 32-year-old Philip Matthews became besotted with the household's young parlourmaid Charlotte Maloney who came from Portsmouth. At the time Matthews was married to his second wife, Maria, with a four-year-old daughter, Elsie, by his late first wife but he somehow managed to convince the naive Charlotte that neither wife nor daughter were really his. Thus using the name Philip Burt, he bigamously married his new love at Salisbury in March 1896. Then Matthews learned that Maria, in revenge for his desertion of her, was threatening to put little Elsie in the workhouse. This was more than he could take and on Easter Monday, 6 April 1896, he left Teignmouth with Elsie under one arm and a paper parcel under the other, announcing that he was taking the girl to a place where she would be cared for. Late that night, 150 miles away at Baffins Farm, the sound of a child's screams set the farm's dogs barking. The next day, a farmworker found Elsie dead in a ditch near Baffins Pond at the front of the farmhouse. She had been strangled. Matthews claimed that Elsie had died of fright after hearing the dogs but he was found guilty of murder and hanged.

Portsmouth: The John Barleycorn, Commercial Road

Sixty-three-year-old widow Mrs Rose Ada Robinson lived alone above the John Barleycorn public house which she had run for 40 years. On 29 November 1943, she was found strangled in her bedroom, the victim of old lag Harold Loughans who had heard whispers that Mrs Robinson kept £2,000 on the premises. When the pub had closed for the night, Loughans had climbed a wall and broken in through a window, only to be surprised by Mrs Robinson. He killed her just to stop her screaming. Charged with murder, Loughans produced three witnesses in court who swore that he was at London's Warren Street underground station at the time of the murder. He was found not guilty but, confronted with terminal cancer, he finally confessed to the murder to the *People* newspaper in 1963. Harold Loughans died two years later.

Southampton: 42 Grove Street

Vivian Messiter, aged 58, worked from a garage at 42 Grove Street as an agent for an oil company. He disappeared on 30 October 1928 and was not heard of again until the following January when his decomposed body, chewed by rats, was found behind some boxes in the locked garage. His killer was William Podmore who had worked for Messiter and had been involved in a swindle concerning bogus orders. Messiter had uncovered the scam and threatened to call the police whereupon Podmore, already wanted by the authorities in Manchester for car theft, battered him to death with a heavy hammer. He then locked the garage and stole Messiter's car to take his lady friend, one 'Golden-haired Lil' for a drive. This ruthless act helped send Podmore to the gallows at Winchester on 22 April 1930.

Winchfield

Lance-corporals are clearly a breed to avoid in Hampshire for, following in the murderous footsteps of Albert Dearnley and Jack Goldenberg came Arthur Mortimer who embarked on a manic two-day spree of calculated motoring mayhem on 7 and 8 August 1935 in which he hit four female cyclists with his car, killing one. On the 7th, he had forced Mrs Alice Series off the road into a ditch and then punched her repeatedly but worse was to follow the next day when he deliberately drove into 20-year-old Phyllis Oakes at Winchfield. She was hurled from her bicycle, bounced off the bonnet of Mortimer's car and landed on a railway bridge, her injuries proving fatal. The car had been stolen from Farnborough and was later abandoned at Ash Common near Aldershot. Having switched cars, Mortimer proceeded to knock another hapless cyclist unconscious near Knaphill in Surrey before a police chase ended in him crashing into a parked van near Guildford. At his trial, it was revealed that Mortimer had suffered severe epileptic fits since falling into a quarry at the age of 12 and his subsequent death sentence was commuted to life.

KENT

Aldington: Pantiles Bungalow

Belgian-born Alice Buxton lived with Hubert Buxton, the man she called her husband, at isolated Pantiles Bungalow, situated off Frith Road to the east of the village of Aldington, between Ashford and Hythe. He was a gardener at nearby Pantiles House while she worked as a waitress at a Folkestone hotel. She also had a secret lover, Polish labourer Hendryk Neimasz, who lived three miles away at Mersham, a situation complicated by the fact that Neimasz and his wife were both friendly with the Buxtons. On the night of 12 May 1961, Neimasz arrived by car at Pantiles Bungalow at around 10 pm but it seems that Hubert had just stumbled across a love letter from Neimasz to Alice who in turn had said she wanted to end the affair. Whatever happened, Neimasz returned quietly an hour later by bicycle and armed with a shotgun. He shot Hubert dead through the scullery window and when Alice, who was getting ready for bed, rushed out of the house in fright, he attacked her in the porch, smashing the gun down on her head. She too died and Neimasz, the wounded lover, was duly executed.

Bromley: 13 College Road

By 1969, this rambling Victorian house had been divided into flats with 35-year-old chauffeur Colin

Saunders and 19-year-old Stanley Wrenn sharing a ground floor room at the front. Saunders, who had convictions for importuning and gross indecency, had offered Wrenn a roof over his head but the latter quickly tired of the arrangement, particularly when he discovered that Saunders had infected him with gonorrhoea. Wrenn decided to kill him and at 5 am on 26 November 1969, he hit Saunders over the head with a gas-ring and then stabbed him repeatedly with a fisherman's knife. Next Wrenn respectfully pulled a sheet over the corpse's head and went through the dead man's possessions before making his escape. He tried to leave in Saunders' employer's car but was involved in an accident almost immediately and was thus forced to walk to Bromley North railway station to catch a train to London. There Wrenn soon gave himself up and was jailed for life. He was released in 1980.

Chatham: nr Sharsted Road, Luton

Alan Poole was a young hoodlum who had deserted from the army, taking a sten gun with him. On 6 June 1951, he returned to his home town of Chatham but before going to his parents' house, he broke into surrounding farms for shelter and food, accompanied by two girls. That evening at the former Corporation Rubbish Dump near Sharsted Road (now called Shawstead Road), Sergeant William Langford and PC Alan Baxter arrived to investigate a report from a man who said he had been shot at Sharsted Farm. Suddenly, Poole and the girls rushed from a nearby hut. Poole turned his gun on the two officers, as a result of which PC Baxter, who was sitting in the squad car, died later in hospital. Poole fled to his parents' home at 114 Symons Avenue and hid in the attic. Shots were fired and the police put tear gas into the letter box before finally storming the house. They found Alan Poole dead, shot by return of fire.

Cobham: Halfpence Lane, Cobham Park

Apothecary Robert Dadd and his talented artist son Richard were staying at the Ship in Cobham for the night of 28 August 1843. Some time after 9 pm, fortified by a few drinks, they went for a walk to Cobham Park and reached a gravel pit about 30 yards inside the park, just off Halfpence Lane. There, Robert Dadd, feeling the effects of the ale, turned towards a tree and started unbuttoning his trousers to relieve himself but as he did so, Richard, totally without warning, launched into a frenzied attack. Robert slumped to the ground whereupon Richard dragged him under the trees and attempted to cut his father's throat with a large razor taken from his pocket. When that failed, he produced a large seaman's knife and thrust it into his father's lung to a depth of four inches. Richard fled to France where he claimed he had carried out the murder under orders from the ancient Egyptian god Osiris. After a similar attack on the continent, he was returned to England and spent the remainder of his life in Broadmoor where he died in 1886. Incidentally, the hollow where the body of Robert Dadd was found is still known locally as Dadd's hole.

Dartford Heath

A secluded area of moorland just some 16 miles from the centre of London, Dartford Heath is seemingly a popular venue for courting couples and murderers alike. On 11

April 1930, young Edith May Parker was crossing Dartford Heath when she was fatally stabbed in the back by 23-year-old Albert Marjeram. The killer's mother insisted that her son was insane and pointed out that as a child he was so violent that he had to be tied down. However the jury decided that he was totally sane when he killed Edith and found him guilty of murder. Marjeram was executed at Wandsworth Prison.

Dartford Heath

Another body was discovered on the Heath in 1957, the tragic outcome of a Latvian love triangle. Car mechanic Janis Abolins and cabinet-maker Vilis Ozolins were best friends but they both loved the same girl, 28-year-old nurse Juasma Kadege, known to all as Kitty. There seemed some debate as to which of the two suitors had won Kitty's heart (perhaps she was confused over their similar-sounding names) but Ozolins became convinced that Abolins had stolen her from him. On 12 February 1957, Ozolins lured his love rival to a garage in Tottenham where he coshed him over the head and ran him over. Ozolins then drove the body to Dartford Heath, stopping at a dentist on the way in an attempt to acquire an alibi. Partly concealed by a gorse bush, Abolins' body was found on a lonely roadside. Beneath the body lay a crumpled mackintosh. It was this which was to prove Ozolins' downfall for he had tried to make the death look like a hit and run, but although it had been raining heavily on Dartford Heath that day, the back of the mackintosh was dry. For this mistake, Ozolins was jailed for life.

Folkestone: 94 Foord Road

By 13 June 1943, 18-year-old cinema usherette Caroline
Trayler had been married for six months. Her husband
was serving in North Africa and, bored with spending
Sunday evenings at home with her mum, she decided to
go to the Mechanics Arms in Folkestone. She left the
pub at closing time with a soldier and was not seen alive
again. When her mother reported her missing, the police
started searching the numerous blitzed buildings in the
town and four days later, they discovered Caroline's
body in a bombed-out shop. She had been strangled and
rough sexual intercourse had taken place shortly before
her death. The forensic trail led to gunner Dennis
Leckey who was subsequently found guilty but an error
by the trial judge in summing up meant that the conviction was quashed and instead of being hanged,
Leckey walked free.

Herne Bay: 80 High Street

The genteel refinement of Herne Bay ideally suited the
purposes of 'Brides in the Bath' murderer George Joseph
Smith who selected the North Kent resort for his first
killing in 1912. Calling himself Henry Williams, he
bigamously 'married' 33-year-old Bessie Mundy at
Weymouth in 1910 before eloping with some of her
money. Two years later, they were reunited by chance
and not only did she forgive him but even agreed to his
suggestion that they should each make a will in favour of
the other. By this time they had moved to a small house
at 80 High Street, Herne Bay, and on 9 July 1912, the
day after the wills had been deposited with a solicitor,
Smith bought a cheap zinc bath from an ironmonger's
shop on the corner of William and Mortimer Streets.

Because it had no taps, he succeeded in getting the price reduced by half a crown. The following day, he took Bessie to a doctor, saying that she had suffered a fit. Gullible Bessie didn't even remember feeling unwell but took her husband's word for it. On 13 July, Smith wrote to the doctor to say his wife was dead. The doctor arrived to find Bessie lying submerged in the bath, clutching a piece of soap in her right hand. Smith gratefully accepted the proceeds of the will and went on to repeat the bath ritual with two new 'brides', Alice Burnham in Blackpool in 1913 and Margaret Lofty at 14 Bismarck Road (now called Waterlow Road), Highgate, London in 1914. Smith was finally brought to justice and hanged at Maidstone Prison on Friday 13 August 1915 — certainly an unlucky day for him!

(† Number 80 High Street, Herne Bay has since been demolished and due to renumbering, its site is now occupied by the shop at 159 High Street.)

King's Wood, Challock Hill, nr Ashford

The glorious summer's day of 3 June 1932 saw the commencement of two separate journeys which were to converge horrifically in a brutal bloodbath at a Kent beauty spot. Early that morning before the sun had risen, 26-year-old Private James Collins went AWOL from his camp at Hythe. Taking his rifle with him, he began the long footslog to London. Meanwhile 69-year-old Janie Swift, her daughter Janie Stemp and grand-daughter Peggy Stemp, set out for a picnic in the silvan setting of King's Wood, when, half a mile from their destination, their sports car passed Collins. Janie Stemp, who was driving, called out a cordial greeting to the weary soldier. Whether or not he was envious of the car is open to speculation but at 1.30 pm he stumbled across their picnic site in the woods and massacred them. Janie Swift and 13-year-old Peggy were shot dead in the car while the body of Janie Stemp was dragged into undergrowth half a mile down the road near the footpath to White Hill. The corpses were spotted by the driver of a Maidstone and District bus travelling along the A251 past King's Wood on his route between Faversham and Ashford. Janie Swift was still grasping the sandwich she had been eating when she was gunned down. Collins fled to London before being overpowered by the police. Eventually he confessed to the murders and was sent to Broadmoor.

Margate: Hotel Metropole

The luxurious Hotel Metropole on the sea-front at Margate served up an unusual murder on 23 October 1929 when 31-year-old homosexual Sidney Fox murdered his mother Rosalind out of sheer greed. The Foxes appeared a typical doting mother and son but they specialised in travelling around the country, swindling high-class hotels. They booked into the Metropole on 16 October and after a few days Sidney asked the manager to move them to a pair of connecting rooms, one of which had a gas fire. Sidney had already taken out accident policies on his mother's life and during the week he made a hasty trip to London to increase them to £3,000. Suddenly at 11.40 pm on the 23rd, Sidney ran downstairs in his shorts, yelling 'Fire!' Mrs Fox was found in her smoke-filled room and died shortly afterwards. The Coroner returned a verdict of accidental death but an eagle-eyed insurance company official noticed that the policies would have expired just 20 minutes after Mrs Fox did.

At his trial it was suggested that Sidney had made his mother drowsy with port and had then either strangled or suffocated her before lighting a fire under her chair with the help of petrol and newspaper. He was found guilty of murder and executed. The Metropole was demolished in the 1930s as part of a road-widening scheme. Its site is now part of a dual carriageway.

SURREY

Ash Vale Station

On the night of 22 August 1952, booking clerk Geoffrey Dean was working late at Ash Vale station, one and a half miles to the north-east of Aldershot. Since the station door was locked and a sign hanging from it announced that all tickets had to be purchased from the porter, none of the passengers using Ash Vale noticed anything amiss and it was not until much later that the porter found 28-year-old Dean lying dead on the floor of the station office, butchered and bearing more than 20 stab wounds. A total of £168 was missing from the safe. Geoffrey Dean's killer was John James Alcott, a former soldier who had befriended the deceased by falsely telling him that he too worked on the railways. It was then that Alcott observed the sizeable amounts of money which were kept in the station safe. He was arrested at a boarding house in Aldershot where the murder weapon was found concealed up the chimney. Alcott's claim that he had suffered a mental blackout at the time of the killing was dismissed and he was found guilty and executed.

Byfleet: Blue Anchor Hotel

Situated on the main road in the centre of Byfleet village is the Blue Anchor Hotel, scene of a celebrated crime of passion in 1924. It centred around Frenchman Jean-Pierre Vaquier who had met Mabel Theresa Jones, wife of the landlord of the Blue Anchor, out in Biarritz and had followed her back to England. Their affair blossomed when Vaquier came to stay at the Blue Anchor, under the pretence that he was waiting payment for the invention of a mincing-machine. Mr Jones was a heavy drinker who regularly took bromo salts the morning after to cure his hangover. On 21 March, waking up from a late-night party at the hotel, Mr Jones went to the bar and downed his salts. Immediately he remarked: 'My God! That was bitter!' Soon he was taken ill and died an agonising death from strychnine poisoning. Police didn't have far to look for the killer. A chemist in London's Southampton Row recognised Vaquier as the customer who had bought strychnine, allegedly for wireless experiments, under the pseudonym of Wanker. Vaquier paid for his love with his life on 12 August 1924.

Croydon: Barlow and Parker's Warehouse, Tamworth Road

On the night of 2 November 1952, 16-year-old Christopher Craig and 19-year-old Derek Bentley set off from their homes in Norbury and caught a 109 bus to West Croydon station. They walked down Tamworth Road as far as Reeves' Corner, crossed over and walked back up to Barlow and Parker's wholesale confectioner's. Both were armed – Craig with a revolver, Bentley with a knife. They waited near the side entrance of the confectioner's and then Craig vaulted the fence, followed by Bentley. But they had been spotted and the police arrived to find the two robbers on the flat roof of the warehouse. Bentley gave himself up but Craig remained defiant, shooting at anything that moved. As PC Sidney Miles kicked the roof door open, Craig summarily shot him in the head. Finally out of ammunition, Craig jumped 25 feet from the roof, fracturing his spine. Although Bentley didn't fire the fatal shot, both were found guilty of murder with considerable controversy surrounding Bentley's alleged remark on the roof: 'Let him have it, Chris.' Craig was too young to hang but Bentley was executed on 28 January 1953.

Croydon: 32 Churchill Road

Cabinet-maker Richard Brinkley was so blinded by his determination to get his hands on an old woman's estate that he succeeded in poisoning the wrong couple. Fifty-one-year-old Brinkley had befriended Johanna Blume, an elderly German woman living in Fulham and had adopted dubious means to become sole beneficiary in her will. Two days after this new will, she died. Her relatives were naturally suspicious about the validity of the document and threatened legal action against Brinkley. Worried that accountant Reginald Parker, who had witnessed the signing, would testify against him, Brinkley decided murder was the only course of action. Parker was lodging at 32 Churchill Road, Croydon, with the Beck family when Brinkley paid him a visit on the evening of 20 April 1907, armed with prussic acid and a bottle of stout. Unfortunately for Brinkley, Parker didn't drink the deadly stout but after the pair had departed, Parker's landlord Richard Beck saw the untouched bottle on the table and poured some for himself and his wife Elizabeth. Both soon died in agony and Brinkley was charged with their murder as well as the attempted murders of Parker and the Becks' daughter Daisy who sipped the lethal cocktail but survived. Brinkley was found guilty and executed at Wandsworth Prison.

Godalming: Surrey County Sanatorium, St Thomas's Hospital, Hydestile

At 43, Margery Radford was a patient in the County Sanatorium at Hydestile, just to the south of Godalming. She was suffering from tuberculosis and her condition was not improved by the belief that her husband Frederick, a laboratory technician at the adjoining St Thomas's Hospital, was trying to poison her. In fact their 14-year marriage was bigamous and Fred had had a string of affairs. Wanting to marry again and convinced that his wife would die soon anyway, he decided to hasten the process by slipping arsenic into the food and fruit parcels he sent her. Mrs Radford had begun to remark how she was often ill after sampling these gifts and gave a selection of fruit pies and plums to a friend for analysis. They were then sent to the medical superintendent at Hydestile but without an accompanying letter of explanation. The superintendent, thinking they were a present, ate them and started vomiting violently. He soon diagnosed that the food contained arsenic. Alas, his discovery was just too late to save Margery Radford who died on 12 April 1949. Before he could be charged, Frederick Radford committed suicide by poisoning himself.

Hankley Common

During an Army exercise on Hankley Common near Godalming on 7 October 1942, two soldiers stumbled across an outstretched human arm protruding from the ground after the surrounding earth had been dislodged by a military vehicle. The decomposed body was that of Joan Pearl Wolfe who had been living rough with 28-

year-old August Sangret, a French-Canadian soldier of Red Indian descent. They had adopted as home a derelict cricket pavilion on the common and also an extremely basic wigwam made of tree branches and sprigs of heather. Sangret killed her on 13 September, stabbing her near a shack on the common with his hook-bladed clasp-knife. Bleeding and terrified, she tried to escape down a hill but fell over a military trip-wire, smashing her front teeth. As she lay on the ground, barely conscious, Sangret rained blows on the back of her head with a heavy silver birch branch. The only possible motive for the murder was that Joan had written to Sangret, informing him that she was pregnant. Sangret was found guilty and hanged at Wandsworth Prison on 29 April 1943.

Hindhead: Moorlands Hotel

Miss Mabel Bundy, a 42-year-old maid at Moorlands Hotel, had spent the latter part of the evening of 4 July 1939 in the bar of the nearby Royal Huts Hotel, a popular venue with soldiers from Thursley Camp. She had left with a Private Smith, followed a little way behind by two of his soldier chums, Boon and Goodwin. Smith walked Mabel to the staff entrance of Moorlands Hotel and it was on the footpath leading to that entrance that her body was found the following morning. She had been attacked with such force that her brain was damaged and she had also been sexually assaulted. Smith claimed she had agreed to have sex with him while Goodwin stated that Boon, who was aggressively drunk, had bent down and struck the woman twice about the face. At the trial, Goodwin was acquitted but

Boon and Smith were found guilty of murder and sentenced to death.

Kenley: Welcomes Stud Farm, Hayes Lane

At the end of the First World War, two former soldiers, Eric Gordon Tombe and Ernest Dyer, went into business together. Following two failures, due in part to Dyer's compulsive gambling, they bought the Welcomes Stud Farm in leafy Hayes Lane at Kenley. Dyer moved in with his family but soon encountered financial difficulty when a suspicious insurance company refused to pay up after the farm was gutted by fire in April 1921. That month Tombe vanished after an argument with Dyer over money. Tombe's bank then received a letter, purporting to be signed by Tombe, allowing Dyer to draw on his account. Dyer proceeded to withdraw Tombe's entire savings (some £2,500), explaining his partner's absence by saying he had eloped with a girl. Then in November 1922, a man calling himself Fitzsimmons was approached at the Old Bar Hotel in Scarborough by police investigating a confidence trick. Fearing arrest, the man shot himself. A search of his hotel room revealed that Fitzsimmons was really Dyer and the cause of his concern came to light when the body of Eric Tombe was found in a well in the grounds of the stud farm. Dyer had shot him in the back of the head.

Merstham Tunnel

The dark secrecy provided by mile-long Merstham Tunnel, eight miles south of Croydon on the London to Brighton line, has twice presented the opportunity for murderers to strike. On 27 June 1881, elderly coin dealer

Isaac Frederick Gold boarded the 2.10pm train from London Bridge to return to his home in Brighton. Alone with him in the carriage was a 22-year-old struggling journalist, Percy Lefroy Mapleton, and when the train reached Merstham tunnel, Lefroy (as he called himself) shot Mr Gold in the neck and stabbed him. He then threw the body out of the train near the entrance to Balcombe Tunnel, south of Crawley. Lefroy left the train at Preston Park on the outskirts of Brighton but was detained by an alert ticket-collector who noticed the passenger's blood-stained clothing. Lefroy told the police that there had been three passengers in the carriage and that when the train had entered Merstham Tunnel, he had heard a shot and been knocked unconscious. But his story crumbled when he was searched and the police found German gold coins of the type in which Mr Gold dealt. Lefroy was hanged on 29 November 1881.

Richmond: 2 Vine Cottages, Park Road

A convicted thief and prostitute, 30-year-old Irishwoman Kate Webster had somehow managed to obtain work as housekeeper to elderly widow Julia Thomas who lived alone at Vine Cottages (subsequently renamed Mayfield) in Richmond. On Sunday 2 March 1879, a fearful quarrel arose between the two women during which Webster hacked Mrs Thomas to death with a cleaver. She then set about dismembering the body on the floor of the scullery before retiring to a public house for refreshment. It was later suggested that she sold jars of human dripping to the landlord! On her return from the hostelry, Webster boiled the remains and, having enlisted the help of an innocent young boy, dumped some portions over Hammersmith Bridge and others over Richmond Bridge. She sold off much of Mrs Thomas's property – even her false teeth for which she received 6s. She began posing as the dead lady but when this ruse was uncovered by a neighbour, Webster fled to Ireland where she was arrested in her home village of Killane, County Wexford, wearing Mrs Thomas's clothes and jewellery. The murderous maid was found guilty and hanged.

Weybridge: The Nook

'The Nook', a grand Edwardian mansion near Brooklands motor racing circuit, was home in 1941 to an elderly recluse, Miss Salmon. One September morning the postman, getting no reply, climbed a ladder to look through her bedroom window and saw Miss Salmon dead on the floor. She had severe head injuries and an attempt had also been made to strangle her. Scattered around the room were the old lady's rifled jewel boxes. The police did not have to look far, for when they arrived they found a drunken sailor, Patrick Cusack, lurching around the front garden, and an equally inebriated Canadian soldier, Peter McDonald, asleep on the kitchen floor. The pockets of both men were full of gems. Cusack blamed McDonald for the murder but a few days before their trial, Cusack died of tuberculosis. McDonald, who until then had remained silent, suddenly found the use of his tongue and laid all the blame at Cusack's door. With Cusack unable to defend himself, McDonald was acquitted and posted back to Canada where he was killed shortly afterwards in a road accident.

Woldingham: The chalk pit off Slines Oak Road

A desolate spot near the North Downs town of Wolding-
ham lent its name to the famous 'Chalkpit Murder' of
1946. The victim was 35-year-old barman John Mudie
who in November was lured from Reigate to the home of
Thomas Ley, former Minister of Justice in New South
Wales, at 5 Beaufort Gardens, off London's Brompton
Road. Ley, 67, had convinced himself that Mudie was
having an affair with his former mistress, Maggie Brook,
and in a fit of jealousy decided that Mudie must be
killed. When Mudie arrived a rug was thrown over his
head, he was trussed in a swivel-chair with a clothes-
line tied around his neck and a French polisher's rag
stuffed into his mouth. Two days later Mudie's body
was found in a chalkpit. He had died of asphyxia. Ley
was charged with murder, along with one of his hired
hands, labourer Lawrence Smith. Both were found
guilty although Smith steadfastly disclaimed responsibility for the killing while Ley simply denied everything.
Ley was committed to Broadmoor, where he died three
months later, and Smith was imprisoned for life.

WEST SUSSEX

Crawley: Giles Yard, Leopold Road

Notorious Acid-Bath Murderer John George Haigh used a small storeroom, rented from a local light engineering firm, off Leopold Road in the old part of Crawley, to carry out his evil machinations. In a secluded yard, the storeroom (which still stands) offered Haigh the privacy necessary for successfully disposing of his victims. Haigh, 39, a soft-spoken charmer, was held in high esteem by his fellow guests at the Onslow Court Hotel in South Kensington where he was staying in 1949. One such guest was wealthy widow Olive Durand-Deacon. He interested her in a proposition to market artificial fingernails and invited her to visit his workshop in Crawley. On 18 February, he drove her there, shot her through the back of the head and stripped her body of all valuables. Haigh then tipped the body into a 40-gallon drum and wearing rubber gloves and an apron, proceeded to fill it with sulphuric acid. As the body began to disintegrate, Haigh pawned his victim's wristwatch for £10 and left other items for valuation. After taking a tea of poached eggs on toast in Crawley, he returned to Kensington and reported Mrs Durand-Deacon as missing. But the police were suspicious of Haigh and when they found he had a previous criminal record, they searched the premises at Giles Yard. Incriminating evidence, including the gun, was found but Haigh boasted: 'Mrs Durand-Deacon no longer exists. I've destroyed her

with acid. You can't prove murder without a body.'
However the confident killer had reckoned without two
items which had survived the acid – an acrylic plastic
denture which was identified as belonging to Mrs
Durand-Deacon, and the strap of her red plastic handbag. Haigh, who had confessed to five other acid-bath
murders (two committed at Crawley), was hanged on 10
August 1949.

Arundel Castle

On the morning of 31 July 1948, librarian Joan Woodhouse told her room-mate at the YMCA Hostel,
Blackheath, that she was going to visit her father in
Barnsley. Instead, for some unknown reason, she
headed in the opposite direction, to the south coast and
Worthing railway station. The following day, 27-year-
old Joan was found strangled and sexually assaulted at
her favourite beauty spot, the wooded grounds of Arundel Castle. She was nearly naked, her clothes resting in a
neat pile some 12 yards from her body. Two years later,
Joan's father successfully applied for a private warrant
to arrest a labourer who lived near Arundel on a murder-
charge, but it was decided that there was insufficient
evidence to send the accused for trial. Joan Woodhouse's murder remains unsolved.

LONDON

LONDON

Balham: The Priory, Bedford Hill

Standing on the northern side of Tooting Bec Common, The Priory (modern address 225 Bedford Hill) is an imposing fortress-like building which in 1876 played host to one of the capital's great unsolved mysteries. It was the home of 30-year-old barrister Charles Bravo and his wife of five months, Florence. On Tuesday 18 April, Charles was taken ill after eating a dinner of whiting, roast lamb and anchovy eggs on toast. Three days later he died, the post-mortem revealing the cause to be antimony poisoning. Suspicion immediately fell upon Florence and her constant companion, widowed governess Jane Cox. Florence had been the mistress of an ageing Malvern doctor, James Gully, but had promised Charles that she would end the affair before the wedding. She had also been left £40,000 by her first husband. And Mrs Cox, who said that Charles had told her just before his death that he had taken poison, had openly argued with her mistress's husband. The Coroner's jury ruled that Charles Bravo had been wilfully murdered but decreed that there was 'insufficient evidence to fix the guilt upon any person or persons.' Florence Bravo died of alcoholism just two years later and maybe with her went the key to the Balham mystery.

Bayswater: Whiteley's Department Store, 55-57 Westbourne Grove

William Whiteley, the 75-year-old founder of Britain's first department store, cultivated a God-fearing image and described himself as the 'Universal Provider'. Unfortunately his public persona was rather at odds with his private behaviour for he failed to provide adequately for his clandestine, illegitimate son. The name of the child was Horace Rayner and on 24 January 1907, he marched into Whiteley's office and demanded an interview with the great man. Whiteley displayed characteristic indifference upon which 27-year-old Rayner shot him dead at point blank range. Rayner then turned the gun on himself and lost an eye in the process. When the full story of Whiteley's hypocrisy became known, there was widespread sympathy for the defendant and although he was found guilty of murder, he was reprieved and served just 12 years in prison.

Bayswater: 21 Leinster Square

In 1958, the basement flat at 21 Leinster Square was occupied by 34-year-old Polish art student Ginter Widra and his girlfriend Shirley Allen who was ten years younger. Widra was paranoid and jealous, and suspected Shirley of posing for pornographic pictures. On the morning of Saturday 4 May 1957 Widra lost his temper and attacked Shirley with a standard lamp before plunging a Japanese samurai sword into her chest. When landlady Doreen Dally attempted to intervene, Widra wounded her too. He then tried to commit suicide by slashing his wrists with a bread-knife. Widra was found guilty of manslaughter and sent to Broadmoor.

Belgravia: 46 Lower Belgrave Street

Just around the corner from Victoria station and leading off Buckingham Palace Road is fashionable Lower Belgrave Street, setting for the infamous Lord Lucan case. Richard John Bingham, seventh Earl of Lucan, was a compulsive gambler who had separated from his wife Veronica in 1973. She remained with the children at 46 Lower Belgrave Street while he frittered away his money at the tables, blaming all his bad luck and the loss of his children on his estranged wife. It seems that he had decided that his fortunes wouldn't change until Veronica was dead. He chose a Thursday night, 7 November 1974, because he thought that it was the nanny's night off. But Sandra Rivett, 29, did not go out that night and was battered to death in the basement breakfast room with a nine-inch length of lead piping wrapped in Elastoplast. When Lady Lucan went downstairs to investigate Sandra's whereabouts, she was attacked in the darkened hall and her assailant put three gloved fingers down her throat, telling her to shut up. She later said: 'I recognised the voice as that of my husband. As I fought back, he attempted to strangle me and then to gouge out my left eye with his thumb.' She fought him off by grabbing his genitals and then he told her that the nanny was dead, adding: 'She is downstairs – but don't look. She is a horrid sight – an awful mess.' Lady Lucan escaped to raise the alarm at The Plumbers' Arms and her husband vanished never to be seen again. His car was found near Newhaven in Sussex with a length of lead piping in the boot.

Bloomsbury: 101 Charlotte Street

Belgian butcher Louis Voisin lived in the basement at
101 Charlotte Street and was more than a little friendly
with Mme Emilienne Gerard who lived half a mile away
at 50 Munster Square, to the east of Regent's Park. Seek-
ing refuge from a Zeppelin raid on the night of 31
October 1917, Mme Gerard journeyed to Voisin's flat,
only to find him in the arms of one Berthe Roche. Each
woman had been blissfully unaware of the other's existence and there was a fierce row between the two during
which Roche struck out at Mme Gerard with a poker and
killed her. Voisin then used his butcher's expertise to
dissect the body before wrapping the pieces up, driving
across Bloomsbury in his cart and dumping them inside
the railings of the central garden of Regent Square, just
south of St Pancras station. The grisly remains were
found by a roadsweeper. A bloodstained sheet, in which
the trunk and arms were concealed, bore a laundry mark
which led the police to Mme Gerard and in turn to Voisin. A search of the Charlotte Street cellar produced
Mme Gerard's head and hands. Voisin was hanged and
Roche sentenced to seven years but she quickly went
mad and within two years she also was dead.

Bow: Eastern Palace Cinema, Bow Road

Nineteen-year-old John Stockwell decided to rob his
workplace, the now defunct Eastern Palace Cinema.
Thus, in the early hours of 7 August 1934, he made his
way to the office of the cinema manager, Dudley Hoard,
felled him with an axe and escaped with £90 from the
safe. When the cleaners reported for duty a few hours
later, they discovered the severely wounded Mr Hoard
behind the upper circle. He died in hospital. Meanwhile

Stockwell put the stolen cash into a suitcase which he left at Aldgate East station and caught a train to the Suffolk resort of Lowestoft. He then faked his own suicide by depositing his clothes on the sands at Great Yarmouth together with his Post Office Savings Book. But the alert manager of the Metropole at Yarmouth became suspicious when his strange guest wrote his address as Luton, Herts instead of Beds. The manager notified the police and the young cinema attendant was arrested, convicted of murder and hanged, foiled by a lousy script.

Brixton: Baytree Road

On the evening of 9 May 1923, taxi driver Jacob Dickey took an ordinary fare from the Trocadero, Piccadilly Circus, to quiet suburban Baytree Road off Acre Lane in Brixton. The cab stopped at the top of Baytree Road at 9.45 pm and a struggle ensued during which Dickey was fatally shot. The murder weapon was abandoned in the road close to Acre Lane and an unusual gold-topped walking-stick, traced to young criminal 'Eddie' Vivian, was found beside the body. After the shooting, a man climbed into the garden of 28 Baytree Road and ran along the back wall until he emerged at 15 Acre Lane, having first sought permission from the occupants to pass through their house. The fleeing man was 22-year-old Alexander 'Scottie' Mason. He denied shooting the taxi driver but was implicated by his criminal associate, Vivian, who said he had lent Mason the stick. After an unsuccessful attempt to put the blame on Vivian, Mason was found guilty and he was sentenced to life. Released in 1937, he died in World War Two, serving with the Merchant Navy.

Camden Town: 2 Priory Street

Tucked around the corner from Camden Road station is Ivor Street. Back in 1890, when it was known as Priory Street, this humble little thoroughfare was at the centre of a sensational murder case involving 24-year-old Eleanor Pearcey who lived at No.2. Pearcey was having an affair with a young married man, Frank Hogg, and on 24 October, she invited Hogg's wife Phoebe to tea. There in the kitchen, she battered Mrs Hogg over the head with a poker and slit her throat. She also killed the Hoggs' 18-month-old daughter. When it was dark, Pearcey loaded the bodies into the baby's pram and set off on a six-mile round journey. She dumped Mrs Hogg's body two miles away at Crossfield Road, Swiss Cottage and disposed of the baby further along Finchley Road, at Cock and Hoop Field, at the junction of West End Lane and Cannon Hill. Finally, she abandoned the pram outside 34 Hamilton Terrace (which runs parallel to Maida Vale) before returning home. Questioned by the police, Pearcey attempted to explain away her bloodstained kitchen by saying she had been killing mice but witnesses testified to hearing screams coming from the house and to seeing Pearcey pushing a pram on the night in question. The jealous mistress was found guilty of murder and duly executed.

Charing Cross Station

The left-luggage cloakroom at Charing Cross station provided an inauspicious resting place for Minnie Bonati, hacked into pieces by the Charing Cross Trunk Murderer, John Robinson. The estranged wife of an Italian waiter, Minnie was free with her favours and accosted businessman Robinson at Victoria station on 4 May 1927. He took her to his third-floor office at 86 Rochester Row (virtually opposite the police station) but when he refused to pay her in return for her personal services, she became violent. In the resulting fracas, she sustained a blow and was suffocated. Robinson then went out and bought a chef's knife (coincidentally from the same shop in Victoria Street that Patrick Mahon had purchased the knife to dismember Emily Kaye three years earlier) and cut the body into five pieces which he deposited in a trunk at Charing Cross station. The discovery of its contents eventually led police to Robinson's office where, although there was no obvious sign of a struggle, an intense search unearthed a blood-stained matchstick in a waste paper basket. This was enough to convict Robinson and he was hanged.

Clapham Common

On New Year's morning 1911, the body of 48-year-old Russian Jew Leon Beron was found on Clapham Common in a clump of gorse bushes near the footpath which leads to Battersea Rise. It seemed the body had been dragged a short distance so that the murder could be completed at a particularly remote spot. Beron had suffered a fractured skull from being struck on the head with a blunt instrument and had then been stabbed in the chest three times while he lay dead on the ground. The letter 'S' had been roughly slashed on each cheek. The man convicted of his murder was fellow Russian Jew and professional burglar, Stinie Morrison, who had spent New Year's Eve with Beron at the Warsaw Restaurant at 32 Osborn Street, Whitechapel. Rumours were rife during the trial that Beron was killed because he was a police informant who had betrayed the anarchists involved in the recent Houndsditch murders and that the cuts on his cheeks signified 'S' for 'spy'. His death sentence commuted to life imprisonment, Morrison protested his innocence to the last, dying in 1921 after going on hunger strike at Parkhurst Prison.

Covent Garden Theatre

Outside the old Covent Garden Theatre (at the side of the present Royal Opera House), Martha Ray, mistress of the fourth Earl of Sandwich, was shot dead on the evening of 7 April 1779 as she was stepping into her carriage after watching a performance of *Love in a Village*. Her assassin was young clergyman James Hackman, rendered an emotional wreck after learning that Martha, with whom he had enjoyed an ongoing affair, would never leave the old Earl. Hackman travelled to London from his new parsonage in Norfolk, fortified by brandy, and with two pistols hidden in his pocket, followed Martha to the theatre. He waited at the nearby Bedford Coffee House until Martha emerged from the theatre at 11 pm when he pushed through the crowds and shot her in the head. Hackman turned the second gun on himself but his suicide attempt failed. The hangman proved more successful.

Cricklewood: 195 Melrose Avenue

Turn off Cricklewood Broadway into Chichele Road and at the junction with Walm Lane you find Melrose Avenue, a rambling stretch of Victorian suburbia now as infamous as Hilldrop Crescent or Rillington Place. For between 1976 and 1981, the front ground-floor flat at No.

195 was rented by former policeman turned civil servant Dennis Nilsen and it was here that he murdered 12 of his 15 victims. Nilsen, a homosexual, began his homicidal orgy on 31 December 1978. The previous evening he had met a young Irishman at the Cricklewood Arms and invited him back to Melrose Avenue. They drank through the night and went to bed together. At dawn on the 31st, Nilsen woke up, looked at the young man lying next to him and strangled him. Nilsen later wrote: 'I was afraid to wake him in case he left me.' Most of the unfortunates he killed were dismembered and stored beneath the living-room floorboards before being burnt in the garden. At one time, there were no fewer than six corpses in the flat as well as bit and pieces in the garden shed. In 1981, Nilsen was offered £1,000 by a developer to move out and he transferred his activities to 23 Cranley Gardens. When police finally searched the garden of 195 Melrose Avenue two years later, they discovered over 1,000 items of human bone.

Golders Green: 620b Finchley Road

At his flat above a greengrocer's, near Golders Green tube station, 39-year-old racketeer Donald Hume murdered his occasional partner-in-crime Stanley Setty on the evening of 4 October 1949. Hume's reasons for doing so were two-fold – he wanted the £1,000 that Setty was carrying but he also sought retribution for the fact that Setty had once kicked Hume's dog. Conceding considerable weight advantage to the burly Setty, Hume set about relaxing his intended victim before suddenly swooping on him with a noose made from a length of window cord. Setty managed to struggle free but Hume ran into the hall and finished him off with a German dagger. Sadly for Hume, the stab wounds had left bloodstains on many of Setty's bank notes and he could only use £100. Hume cleaned up the flat and hid the body in the coal cupboard before chopping it up into small parcels. A qualified pilot, he then hired a light plane from Elstree Aerodrome and dropped the parcels (weighed down with rubble) into the North Sea. Again Hume was unlucky, having to make one drop too early because of adverse weather conditions with the result that the torso was washed up on the marshes bordering the Blackwater River near Tillingham in Essex. Hume was charged with murder but found not guilty although he was sentenced to 12 years for being an accessory, having concocted a story about dropping the parcels for three mysterious men he had met. On his release in 1958, Hume confessed to Setty's murder and the following year he shot dead a taxi driver in Zurich and was sentenced to life.

Hampstead: The Magdala Tavern, South Hill Park

The Magdala Tavern is where 28-year-old Ruth Ellis, the last woman in Britain to hang, gunned down her lover, racing driver David Blakely. Ellis, a twice-married night club manageress, had been involved in a stormy relationship with Blakely for the previous two years. When he finally tried to free himself from her clutches, she followed him to 29 Tanza Road, Hampstead, where he was staying with friends. Spotting him leaving the house with a pretty young nanny, Ellis decided to end the relationship for good and acquired a revolver. On the evening of Sunday 2 April 1955, she spotted Blakely's grey-green Vanguard van parked outside the saloon bar entrance to the Magdala public house. This is situated at the bottom of South Hill Park, a hilly road leading down to Hampstead Heath station composed of Victorian houses and a few small shops. Wearing heavy, black-rimmed spectacles, she peered through the bar window. Blakely had gone to the Magdala with a friend, Clive Gunnell, to buy a flagon of beer for his hosts at Tanza Road. The pair emerged shortly after 9 pm by which time Ellis was waiting a short way up the hill. As Blakely fumbled for his car keys in the dimly-lit street, Ellis walked towards him, called out 'David' and shot him. He tried to run off but three more shots felled him outside Hanshaw's, a newsagent's next door to the pub. Blakely lay dead, face down on the pavement and his blood, mixed with the beer from the pierced flagon, formed a frothy red river trickling down the gutter. Ellis surrendered quietly and accepted her punishment.

Curiously, the last two women to be hanged in England both committed their crimes in South Hill Park. For on 13 December 1954, Cypriot Styllou Christofi was executed after jealously strangling her daughter-in-law, Hella, at the family home, the ground floor of 11 South Hill Park.

Holloway: 39 Hilldrop Crescent

Curving away from Camden Road near the junction with Brecknock Road, Hilldrop Crescent now boasts a block of flats named Margaret Bondfield House. But on that site, until it was damaged by a Second World War bomb, stood No. 39, a large if gloomy, three-storeyed semi that in 1910 was home to Hawley Harvey Crippen. Calling himself a doctor, although he wasn't qualified to practise in Britain, the impoverished Crippen rented the two lower floors with his wife Cora, a modest music-hall artiste whose professional name was Belle Elmore. Mrs Crippen learned that her husband was having an affair with young typist Ethel Le Neve and threatened to remove their joint savings. Desperate to prevent this, Crippen poisoned his wife with five grains of hyoscine hydrobromide on 1 February 1910 after they had entertained friends. Mrs Crippen was last seen alive waving goodbye from the upstairs parlour window. Crippen explained away her disappearance by saying that she had gone to the United States to care for a sick relative but within two weeks, he had installed Miss Le Neve at 39 Hilldrop Crescent. Then he panicked and fled with his mistress to Canada on the SS Montrose whereupon police searched the house and unearthed the mutilated remains of Mrs Crippen buried beneath the cellar floor. The subsequent dramatic arrest, including Miss Le Neve's attempt to disguise herself as a boy, and the suspicions of the ship's captain and his historic wireless message to Scotland Yard, have been well documented. They resulted in Crippen being found guilty of murder and hanged at Pentonville Prison, less than a mile from Hilldrop Crescent.

Islington: 63 Tollington Park

In January 1910, insurance agent Frederick Henry Seddon moved into a 14-roomed semi-detached house at 63 Tollington Park, off Hornsey Road, with his wife Margaret, their five children and his elderly father. In July of that year, he sub-let the top floor to 49-year-old Miss Eliza Barrow who was deaf, dumpy and drunk but who had the redeeming feature in Seddon's eyes of being reasonably wealthy. A former preacher, Seddon was obsessed with money and soon persuaded Miss Barrow to trust his financial judgement. In a little over a year, her fortune had gone and she was dead. She died in agony in her room on 14 September 1911. The death certificate listed the cause as 'epidemic diarrhoea' but in truth she had been poisoned by Seddon with arsenic. Both Seddons were charged but Margaret was acquitted, leaving her arrogant husband to face the hangman.

Islington: 25 Noel Road

Celebrated playwright Joe Orton lived in a small terraced house at 25 Noel Road, Islington, with his lover of over 15 years, fellow writer Kenneth Halliwell. The latter was riddled with insecurity, struggling in the shadow of his partner's success, and had come to the conclusion that Orton was tiring of him. At around midday on 9 August 1967, a chauffeur arrived to take Orton to Twickenham Studios where he was to discuss a film script. Receiving no reply but noticing that the lights were on inside, the chauffeur peered through the letterbox. There he saw the naked body of Halliwell. The police also discovered the body of Orton, lying on the bed, bludgeoned to death with a hammer. In the depths of despair, Halliwell had murdered Orton and then taken his own life.

Lambeth: 103 Lambeth Palace Road

A second-floor room at this address was the headquarters of cross-eyed Scot, Dr Thomas Neill Cream, the Lambeth Poisoner, who concentrated his murderous activities in the seedy area bordered by the River Thames, Blackfriars Road and Lambeth Road. On 20

October 1891, Matilda Clover, a 26-year-old prostitute, suffered an agonising death at 27 Lambeth Road, a house of ill-repute. Before her demise, she spoke of being given pills by a man named Fred, whom she described as tall, dark, moustachioed and wearing a tall silk hat and a cape. Rumours immediately spread that Jack the Ripper was back in town. Matilda had been poisoned with strychnine and the same fate befell two more prostitutes, Emma Shrivell and Alice Marsh, who worked at 118 Stamford Street. Cream, who had already served a life sentence in the United States for strychnine poisoning, was trapped because he tried to incriminate a young medical student, Walter Harper. Cream showed the police a letter, allegedly received by the Stamford Street victims, warning them of a Dr Harper who was threatening to deal with them as he had done Matilda Clover and another prostitute Louise Harvey. But unknown to Cream, Harvey, though given the lethal pills by the demon doctor, had survived. She had only pretended to swallow them and was thus able to shop Cream who was duly hanged on 15 November 1892, having committed at least five murders.

London Zoo

When passions ran high in the rooms above the tapir house, there was only one possible outcome – murder. In the absence of his colleague Mohammad Sayed Ali, who had returned home to Calcutta, Burmese keeper San Dwe enjoyed the additional perks derived from looking after both the London Zoo elephants which gave children's rides. But then Ali returned to Regent's Park in June 1928, and Dwe was returned to relatively menial tasks. Dwe, who shared rooms with Ali above the tapir house near the Outer Circle, bitterly resented giving up his job and extra pay. On 24 August 1928, two passing policemen heard groans from the direction of the tapir house. The found Dwe in a state of disrepair, nursing an injured foot. Inside Ali had been hacked to death with a sledgehammer and a pick axe. In broken English, Dwe tried to blame intruders, but nobody could ascertain why anyone would want to break into the tapir house. With no known tapir-nappers to support his story, Dwe was found guilty and sent back to Burma.

Marylebone: Montagu Place

While Hitler was bombing war-time London, a young RAF cadet, Gordon Frederick Cummins, saw the black-out as the opportunity to carry out a quick-fire series of Ripper-style murders. His carnage began on 9 February 1942 when the strangled body of schoolmistress Evelyn Hamilton was discovered in an air-raid shelter in Montagu Place. The following morning, prostitute Evelyn Oatley was found strangled and mutilated in her flat in Wardour Street, Soho. Next came prostitute Margaret Lowe, horrifically carved up at her flat in Gosfield Street, followed by Doris Jouannet, butchered at her flat at 187 Sussex Gardens, Paddington. The four women had been killed in the space of just five days. While police were investigating the murders, news came through of another attack, on a girl near Piccadilly Circus. Her screams alerted a passer-by and saved her life. She identified her attacker as a young airman and a gas mask dropped nearby in the haste of escape was traced to 28-year-old Cummins. The 'Silk Stocking Murderer' as he became known, because he used nylons to strangle some of his victims, was hanged on 25 June 1942.

Mayfair: 14 Norfolk Street

The murder of Lord William Russell, found dead in his bed with his throat cut at 14 Norfolk Street on the morning of 5 May 1840, greatly disturbed the gentle calm of the aristocracy. By noon, Queen Victoria had been told the news by a saddened Prince Albert. Lord Russell's 23-year-old Swiss valet, Francois Courvoisier, was eventually hanged for the murder but at first the evidence against him was weak since none of his Lordship's stolen valuables had been recovered. While the trial was nearing its conclusion, the part-owner of the Hotel Dieppe, near Leicester Square, happened to read a French newspaper account of the case. He showed it to his cousin who miraculously remembered an incident six weeks previously when a young Swiss, once employed at the hotel, had deposited a parcel with her for safe-keeping. She immediately found and opened the parcel to reveal Lord Russell's missing silver. For Courvoisier this remarkable coincidence proved the case conclusively and the jury found him guilty.

Norfolk Street has since been renamed Dunraven Street but the old number 14 no longer stands. Its site is approximately that of 16 Dunraven Street.

Mayfair: 13 Park Lane

After the death of Lord Russell, there were no further murders in affluent Mayfair until 19 April 1871 when a Frenchwoman, Mme Riel, was found choked to death at her house at 13 Park Lane (the site is now 14 Old Park Lane). Mme Riel had disappeared the previous day but her fate was not revealed until her daughter searched the house. She was curious to find the pantry locked and when she opened it, she found her mother's body with a rope around the neck. The killer was Mme Riel's Belgian cook, 29-year-old Marguerite Diblanc. Her mistress had accused her of eavesdropping and drinking to excess, subsequently dismissing her on only a week's notice. Diblanc demanded a month's pay but Mme Riel, not renowned for her generosity, insisted that she worked her notice. Diblanc then killed her harridan boss and stole money from her safe before fleeing to Paris where she was arrested. She was found guilty of murder but the jury decided that she had been unduly provoked by Mme Riel and she earned a reprieve from the noose.

Muswell Hill: Muswell Lodge, Tetherdown

Now demolished, the once splendid Muswell Lodge stood near the junction of Burlington Road and Tetherdown off Fortis Green. By 1896, it was a decaying mansion, the home of 79-year-old widower Henry Smith who lived in near constant dread of being robbed. Although the house was fitted with alarms and tripwires, his worst fears came true on the night of 13-14 February. Hearing burglars entering through the kitchen window, he went downstairs and was bludgeoned to death with 12 blows to the head. The killers then rifled the safe in his bedroom. The discovery at the murder scene of a child's lantern led the authorities to Albert Milsom who was charged with his partner in crime, the highly aggressive Henry Fowler. During the trial, Fowler actually tried to strangle Milsom and even at their hanging, another prisoner had to be lynched on the beam between them to stop the pair coming to blows!

Muswell Hill: 23 Cranley Gardens

Dennis Nilsen occupied the attic part of 23 Cranley Gardens between October 1981 and February 1983, during which time he murdered three people. The house, a Victorian semi, scruffily painted white and pale blue, stood in quiet Cranley Gardens, off Muswell Hill Road near Highgate Wood. It was here that Nilsen ironically caused his own downfall, complaining that the drains were blocked, having tried to flush pieces of his victims down the lavatory. A plumber came to take a look and found that lumps of rotting flesh were obstructing the pipe outside No. 23. When the flesh was identified as human, the police searched Nilsen's squalid four-roomed flat and in the wardrobe found two plastic sacks, containing two torsos, four arms, one boiled head, one partly boiled head and assorted internal organs. A Sainsbury's bag produced a heart, two lungs, a spleen, a liver, a gall bladder, kidneys and intestines. And the neighbours wondered why the front window at the top of the house was always left wide open ... 'The Murderer of the Century' was sentenced to life and 23 Cranley Gardens was sold in 1984 for a figure considerably below the asking price.

Notting Hill: 10 Rillington Place

Beneath the Westway flyover and behind the Metropolitan Line, just to the west of Ladbroke Grove station, is the spot where, 40 years ago, John Reginald Christie hideously murdered at least six women. Rillington Place itself is long gone. After the trial, its name was changed

by popular demand to Ruston Close but that was demolished in the 1970s. Ruston Mews still exists but probably
the most precise location is Bartle Road. Rillington Place
was a cul-de-sac of small three-storeyed terraced
houses. No 10, a particularly drab building, was divided
into three flats. Christie and his wife Ethel lived on the
ground floor which enjoyed a small garden and use of a
communal washhouse and lavatory, reached only via
Christie's kitchen. Christie's *modus operandi* was to
lure women back to the house, get them drunk, sit them
in a deck chair, intoxicate them with coal gas, then
strangle and rape them. His first victims, student Ruth
Fuerst and spinster Muriel Eady, were killed in 1943 and
1944 respectively while Christie was a special constable
in the War Reserve Police. Both were buried in the garden under cover of darkness and when Ruth Fuerst's
thighbone rose to the surface, Christie used it to prop up
the fence. In 1948, new tenants moved into the top flat –
Welshman Timothy Evans and his pregnant wife Beryl.
There seems little doubt that it was Christie who strangled mother and child and hid the bodies in the
washhouse, leaving the innocent Evans to hang. On 14
December 1950, Christie strangled his wife and buried
her under the floorboards in the front room – the same
makeshift grave in which he had initially placed Ruth
Fuerst. Christie was now an insatiable necrophile and
by February 1951, the bodies of three prostitutes, Kathleen Maloney. Rita Nelson and Hectorina Maclennan,
had been secreted in an alcove behind a cupboard in the
kitchen. The following month Christie decided to move
out, having first papered over the kitchen alcove. On his
first day at 10 Rillington Place the new tenant, looking
for somewhere to fix a bracket, thought the paper-
covered alcove sounded remarkably hollow. He made a

hole and shone a torch into the space behind. In total, police found three women in the alcove, two more in the garden and Ethel Christie under the floorboards. One of the most evil murderers of the 20th Century was finally brought to justice and hanged on 15 July 1953.

Penge: 34 Forbes Road

These days Penge is probably best known for its forma-tion dancing team but back in 1877 this quaintly respectable South London suburb acquired an evil repu-tation following the cruel death of 33-year-old Harriet Staunton in the first-floor bedroom of a house in Forbes Road. Residents were so outraged at the good name of Penge being sullied that the street name was quickly changed to Mosslea Road, by which it is still known today. Wealthy Harriet was married to auctioneer's clerk Louis Stanton who effectively banished her to re-mote Firth Cottage at Cudham in Kent while he pursued an affair with a local girl, Alice Rhodes. Supposedly cared for by Staunton's brother Patrick and sister-in-law Elizabeth, poor Harriet was virtually a prisoner, sleeping on a bed of boards and being slowly starved to death. Fearing that there would be an inquiry if she died at Cudham, the Stauntons arranged for the emaciated Har-riet (by now she could barely walk) to be brought up to London. On the night of 13 April 1877, she was taken on the train to Penge East station and from there Louis carried her to Forbes Road where he had rented two rooms. Within hours she was dead. The three Stauntons and Alice Rhodes were tried for murder. They were sen-tenced to death but at the last moment reprieved, the men receiving prison sentences and the women being freed.

Soho: Café Royal, Regent Street

Even the elegant Café Royal at the bottom end of Regent Street was not above playing host to murder. On the morning of 6 December 1894, nightwatchman Marius Martin was found shot dead just inside the side entry to the Café Royal in Glasshouse Street. There were no signs of a break-in and it was thought that the killer had hidden in the building after it had closed, possibly in the men's lavatory. Police had little to go on, particularly since the deceased had actively enjoyed reporting his colleagues for minor misdemeanours, causing many of them to be dismissed. Not surprisingly, this behaviour had earned him a number of enemies and his murderer was never caught.

Soho: Little Newport Street

Prostitute Suzanne Naylor lived in a flat at Little Newport Street (off Charing Cross Road, just around the corner from Leicester Square) with her ponce, Frenchman George Lacroix. They were owed £25 by one Emile Allard, better known as Red Max Kassel, a Latvian in his late fifties who controlled a number of prostitutes in Soho. Kassel refused to pay up so on 23 January 1936, Lacroix lured him to the flat and shot him six times. The flat was then cleaned up and Kassel's body was driven to St Albans where it was dumped in the grass beside Cell Barnes Lane, on the outskirts of the town. Lacroix fled to Paris where he was sentenced to ten years' hard labour followed by 20 years' expulsion from France.

Soho: Lyons' Corner House, Oxford Street

On the northern side of Oxford Street near the Tottenham Court Road end once stood that haven of good eating, a Lyons' Corner House. Like any other day, 20 April 1945 saw the groundfloor restaurant packed by around 5 pm. At one table sat a family of six, among them 27-year-old Jack Tratsart, bespectacled and unassuming. Suddenly six shots rang out. Customers screamed and dived for cover and three members of the Tratsart family fell to the ground. Jack stood over them, the smoking gun still in his hand. Two died – Jack's Belgian father, John Tratsart, and Jack's epileptic sister Claire. Jack's disabled brother, Hugh, was wounded. Tratsart was revealed to be a manic depressive who hated his father and thought that because of their disabilities, his brother and sister were better off dead too. Earlier in the meal, his aunt had spotted Jack playing with the gun but he told her it was a water-pistol and she carried on chatting and laughing, blissfully unaware of the drama that was about to unfold. Tratsart was declared insane and sent to Broadmoor where he died two years later.

Strand: Savoy Hotel

Wealthy Egyptian playboy Prince Ali Kamel Fahmy Bey booked into the Savoy early in July 1923, with his French wife, Marguerite, and his entourage. They took a suite on the fourth floor with fine views of the river, situated as it was at the rear of the building away from the noisy traffic of the Strand. However Mme Fahmy found it impossible to relax. Her marriage of six months was proving difficult due to her husband's weird sexual desires, and she was convinced that he was plotting to kill her. At the height of a violent thunderstorm just before 2 am on 10 July, Prince Ali returned to his suite. An altercation between the two took place in the corridor and ended in Ali's death from three bullets. At her trial, it was claimed that Mme Fahmy acted in self defence and to much rejoicing she was acquitted.

Strand: Savoy Hotel

A far bloodier though less publicised murder took place at the Savoy on the night of 1 October 1980. Screams were heard coming from Room 853 and the partly-clothed body of prostitute Catherine Russell was discovered within. In a frenzied attack, she had been stabbed 55 times. A diary belonging to Tony Marriott of Horsham, Sussex, was found nearby and Marriott was arrested in Southend where he had been spotted by an alert publican. Marriott, using the pseudonym D. Richards, admitted that he had booked a room at the Savoy expressly with the intention of killing a prostitute. He had phoned Catherine Russell and asked her to come to the hotel. While she was getting ready, he stabbed her. Marriott was committed to Broadmoor.

Waterloo Bridge

Georgi Markov was a 49-year-old Bulgarian working in London for the BBC World Service. On the evening of 7 September 1978, he was waiting to catch his bus home on Waterloo Bridge when he felt a jab in his right thigh from the tip of an umbrella. The man behind him mumbled an apology, dropped the umbrella and ran off. Markov went home but by the following morning his temperature had shot up to 104 degrees and he was vomiting violently. On examining the puncture, he saw that there was blood on his jeans. He died a few days later. A tiny but sophisticated metal pellet was subsequently removed from Markov's thigh and was found to contain a deadly poison, ricin. The motive for Markov's murder was thought to have been to silence his outspoken broadcasts – there had been a similar incident in Paris the previous year but on that occasion the wounded Bulgarian survived the jab.

Whitechapel: 215 Whitechapel Road

Married brushmaker Henry Wainwright, regarded as a pillar of the local community, had tired of his affair with young milliner Harriet Lane. So on 11 November 1874, he shot her three times in the head at his warehouse at 215 Whitechapel Road, backing on to Vine Court, and buried her under the floor. For the next year, Wainwright informed Harriet's relatives that she had gone to France, even cajoling his brother Thomas into sending fake letters purporting to come from Harriet. But then Henry Wainwright's business collapsed and he was force to move premises to the Borough. The terrible stench of the decaying corpse meant that he had to take Harriet with him so he dismembered the body into small parcels to be transported across London by cab. He asked a former workmate, Alfred Stokes, to help but while Wainwright was away summoning a cab, Stokes glanced inside one of the parcels and spotted a human hand. Henry Wainwright was duly arrested and hanged while his brother Thomas received seven years in prison for being an accessory after the fact.

Whitechapel: Miller's Court

Mary Kelly, Jack the Ripper's fifth and final victim, was found horrifically butchered on 9 November 1888 at her grim lodgings at Room 13, Miller's Court, Dorset Street, a narrow thoroughfare off Commercial Street. She was the only one of the Ripper's victims not to die in the streets, having unwisely invited him into her room. For there, free from interruption, the Ripper carried out his most hideous attack of all. The Police News was candid in its report of the find: 'Such a shocking state of things was there as has probably never been equalled in the annals of crime . . . The throat had been cut right across with a knife, nearly severing the head from the body. The abdomen had been ripped partially open, and both of the breasts had been cut from the body . . . The abdomen had been slashed with a knife across and downwards, and the liver and entrails wrenched away. The entrails and other portions of the frame were missing, but the liver, etc, it is said, were found placed between the feet of his poor victim. The flesh from the thighs and legs, together with the breasts and nose, had been placed by the murderer on the table, and one of the hands of the dead woman had been pushed into her own stomach.'

Dorset Street is now Duval Street (just to the north of White's Row on the west side of Commercial Street) while Miller's Court itself is buried under a car park near Spitalfields Market. Across Commercial Street is the Jack the Ripper public house which Mary Kelley frequented when it was called the Ten Bells. What of the other Ripper venues? Bucks Row (where Mary Anne Nicholls was killed) is now Durward Street, just around the back of Whitechapel tube station; 29 Hanbury Street (Annie Chapman) was rebuilt as part of Truman's brewery; Berner Street (Elizabeth Stride) is now Henriques

Street and Mitre Square (Catherine Eddowes) still exists to this day, just inside the City of Aldgate.

Whitechapel: The Blind Beggar, Whitechapel Road

Standing near the junction with Cambridge Heath Road, the Blind Beggar achieved overnight notoriety after Ronnie Kray gunned down George Cornell on 8 March 1966. Cornell was a member of the rival Richardson gang from South London and unwisely decided to stray on to the Krays' territory. Previously, he had also insulted Ronnie so when Kray, drinking in the Lion in Tapp Street, heard that Cornell was nearby at the Blind Beggar, he and a friend resolved to settle the score. As Cornell sat in the saloon with two companions it is ironic that the juke-box was playing 'The Sun Ain't Gonna Shine Anymore', for Ronnie strode in and shot him between the eyes. Apparently, nobody saw a thing. Reggie Kray, like his twin, featured prominently in the murder stakes by stabbing small-time hoodlum Jack 'The Hat' McVitie to death at a basement flat in 1 Evering Road, Stoke Newington. The Krays finally stood trial at the Old Bailey in 1969 for the double murder of Cornell and McVitie. Both were found guilty and sentenced to life imprisonment.

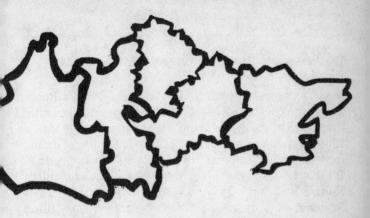

HOME
COUNTIES

BEDFORDSHIRE

Deadman's Hill, nr Clophill

The scene of the famous A6 murder of 1961. On the evening of 22 August, 38-year-old married man Michael Gregsten and his lover, 23-year-old Valerie Storie, were sitting in Gregsten's grey Morris Minor by a Thames-side cornfield at Dorney Reach between Windsor and Maidenhead. Gregsten and Storie worked together at a research laboratory in Slough. Suddenly they were threatened by a man with a gun. He climbed into the back seat and forced Gregsten to drive some 30 miles before ordering him to pull into a lay-by at the top of Deadman's Hill on the A6 just south of Clophill. The gunman asked for a duffle bag to be handed to him but as Gregsten moved, he was killed by two shots to the head. The gunman then forced Storie into the back seat where he raped her and shot her several times before driving off. The car was later abandoned in Ilford and the murder weapon was found tucked under an upstairs seat on a London bus. Though paralysed, Storie survived and was able to identify petty criminal James Hanratty as the murderer. Despite protesting his innocence to the bitter end, Hanratty was hanged at Bedford on 4 April 1963 but the controversy surrounding his conviction still continues.

Leighton Buzzard: The Firs

Ruby Keen and Leslie Stone had known each other for six years but when Stone joined the army and was posted to Hong Kong, their relationship cooled. Ruby had no shortage of admirers and several were keen to take Stone's place in her affections. She became engaged to a local police constable but her new life was suddenly disrupted by Stone's early discharge from the army on medical grounds at the end of 1936. Stone, who lived in the hamlet of Heath and Reach, a mile north of Ruby's home at Plantation Road, Leighton Buzzard, was anxious for a reconciliation with his former love and on Sunday 11 April 1937, he took her for a drink in Leighton Buzzard. They finished up at the Stag Hotel before walking past Plantation Road and into a quiet lovers' lane, The Firs, on the outskirts of town about 300 yards from Ruby's home. The body of 23-year-old Ruby was found there at 7 am the following morning by a railwayman making his way to work. Stone claimed they had quarrelled and that Ruby had hit him. He responded by strangling her with her own black silk scarf, her clothing being ripped to shreds as she valiantly fought for her life. Stone was hanged on Friday 13 August 1937.

Luton: 14 Regent Street

Investigations into the Luton Sack Murder, as it became known, began on the foggy afternoon of 19 November 1943 when workmen spotted a sack in the shallow River Lea near the Vauxhall motor works. It contained the naked body of a pregnant woman whose face was so badly battered it was impossible to put a name to her. Even her teeth had been removed in order to prevent dental identification. Photographs of the corpse screened at local cinemas also failed to elicit any positive response. Then, three months after the gruesome discovery, a dog dug up a piece of cloth on nearby wasteland. The cloth was traced to a Mrs Manton of 14 Regent Street, Luton, situated just below the present-day Chapel Viaduct. Her husband, a former boxer by the name of Horace William 'Bertie' Manton, maintained that she was living in London but police noticed an uncanny resemblance between Manton's daughter and the dead woman. Eventually a thumb print taken from the kitchen at Regent Street proved conclusively that Mrs Caroline Manton was the victim. Then the truth came out. Manton had killed her on 18 November in the course of a heated argument – they regularly quarrelled about her friendship with soldiers. He hit her repeatedly with a heavy wooden stool then, realising she was dead, he undressed her, tied her up in plastic sacks, carried her down to the cellar and cleaned up before the children came home for tea. When it was dark and the children had gone out again, he laid the wrapped body across the handlebars of his bicycle, wheeled it down to the river and rolled it in. Manton was found guilty of murder but his death sentence was commuted to life imprisonment. In the event, he died in Parkhurst Prison in 1947.

BUCKINGHAMSHIRE

Bledlow Ridge: Lambourne House

Five miles north-west of High Wycombe lies the Chiltern village of Bledlow Ridge where one of the most prominent residences is Lambourne House, tastefully converted from a series of farm buildings. In 1983, it was home to 32-year-old Michael Telling, a member of the wealthy Vestey family, and his American second wife Monika. Bisexual, a drug addict and an alcoholic, Monika made it clear that her main interest in Telling was his money. She made his life a misery, even teaching their pet cockatoo to say, 'Piss off, Michael'. On Tuesday 29 March 1983, Telling was due to enter hospital for a check on his mental condition. That morning, with Monika showing her customary lack of compassion, Telling calmly went to the bedroom and returned to the living room carrying a rifle which he had recently brought back from a trip to Australia. He leaned it against the wall but as Monika approached him, he picked up the rifle and shot her three times. Overcome with grief, he apologised to the corpse before dragging it into the spare room. The body remained in an outhouse until August (meanwhile Telling told friends that Monika had finally left him) when Telling was forced to move it. He transported the body down to Haldon Hill, overlooking the Devon and Exeter racecourse, where he hacked off the head and propped the torso against a tree. The headless corpse was discovered by a startled motorist who had stopped to answer nature's call. It would appear that Telling couldn't bear to be parted from Monika's head which he kept in a polythene bag in the boot of his Mini together with a can of live maggots from an anglers' shop in Marlow. When the whole sad tale was uncovered, Telling was found guilty of manslaughter, by reason of diminished responsibility.

Denham Village

Situated on the outskirts of London, Denham has long had associations with the film industry but few horror movies would be able to match the carnage that occurred in the quiet village one night in May 1870 when a tramp butchered an entire family. John Owen was a drifter who had briefly worked for the village blacksmith, Emmanuel Marshall, but had been disgruntled about what he considered to be his paltry wages. His resentment grew to the point where he broke into Marshall's isolated house, wielding the blacksmith's own sledgehammer, and smashed the skulls of Marshall, his wife, his mother, his sister and three of his children. Mercifully, two other children were away from home. On his way out, Owen defiantly smashed a portrait of the blacksmith. As he was leaving the house, Owen encountered a neighbour and told her he was Marshall's brother. However she was able to give the police a good description and Owen was brought to justice for his savagery and hanged.

ESSEX

Braintree: The Barn Restaurant

In the small hours of 5 November 1972, two men broke into the Barn Restaurant at Braintree and demanded the keys to the safe. When owner Bob Patience refused, one of the men shot him, his daughter Beverley and wife Muriel. Muriel Patience died from her injuries. The raiders escaped with £900. Londoner George Ince stood accused twice – on the first occasion no verdict was reached and at a second trial he was found not guilty. Then in June 1973, police were told that a worker at a hotel in the Lake District had shown a man a gun which he said had been used in the murder. The worker was 30-year-old John Brook and the murder weapon was found sewn into the mattress of his bed. So, at a third trial in January 1974, Brook was sentenced to life imprisonment for murder and attempted murder while his accomplice, Nicholas de Clare Johnson, who insisted that Brook alone had carried out the shootings, was jailed for ten years for manslaughter.

Clavering, nr Saffron Walden: Moat Farm

Like many before her, Camille Holland, a somewhat naive 55-year-old spinster with an accumulated fortune of £7,000, was captivated by the dubious charm of forger and womaniser Samuel Herbert Dougal. In April 1899, they moved into a lonely farmhouse (which still stands today) near Clavering, some six miles south-west of Saffron Walden. The small house was situated at the end of a cart-track, leading off several rarely-used lanes, and was surrounded by dark fir trees. Dougal named it Moat Farm since the house was circled by a stagnant moat which could only be crossed by a bridge. A more suitable setting for murder is hard to imagine. No sooner had they taken up residence there than Dougal was caught trying to seduce a maid. Camille ordered him to leave. This obviously made it impossible for Dougal to gain access to her fortune, which he estimated at ten times its true worth, so Dougal decided to murder the hapless Miss Holland. On 19 May, they went shopping in Saffron Walden in a horse and trap. They were seen driving over the bridge from Moat Farm but Dougal then stopped the trap, shot Camille in the head and crept back to the farm. He covered the body with blackthorn as a temporary measure until under the safe cover of darkness, he spent the entire night burying her in a drainage ditch. Camille's body remained there for four years while Dougal financed his entertainment of a string of women at Moat Farm by forging Camille's signature on cheques. When he was finally arrested for forgery, a search of the farm unearthed Camille's body. Samuel Dougal, the Moat Farm murderer, was executed at Chelmsford on 14 July 1903.

Dagenham: Eastbrook End

Dagenham in the 19th Century was rather more rural than it is today. It was a district of fields and ditches, an eerie place to be at night, especially when a mist was drifting across from the Thames. Young PC George Clark's beat took him along some typically lonely stretches and it was in an isolated cornfield in the early hours of 30 June 1846 that his body was discovered with severe head wounds. His bloodstained cutlass was lying in a nearby hedge-bank. The case remained unsolved for 12 years until a Mrs Page came forward to say that her late husband William had committed the murder with three other men – Ned Wood, George Chalk and George Blewett. She said the gang had killed Clark after he had disturbed them stealing corn. But by 1858, Page was dead, Wood had hanged himself and Chalk was thought to be in Australia, leaving just Blewett to face the consequences. He was charged but freed. And the Dagenham police-killer was never brought to justice.

Epping Forest

Ten miles north-west of the centre of London, Epping Forest, once the haunt of Dick Turpin, has always been a popular destination for courting couples. But one lovers' tryst ended in cold-blooded murder on a November evening in 1952. On leave from the RAF, Kenneth Dolden had gone to the forest with his fiancée, Jacynth Bland. Dolden parked his car in a suitably romantic glade and was sitting in the back seat with Miss Bland when the door was suddenly wrenched open by a modern highwayman, wearing a grey cloth cap pulled down over his eyes and with a handkerchief masking his lower face. Thinking the masked man was trying to steal the car, Dolden told him to clear off but the man responded by shooting him three times. Dolden managed to stagger out of the car but died in hospital. No plausible motive was ever found for the killing and the murderer was never apprehended.

Higham's Park

Thirty years earlier, another murder had taken place on the edge of Epping Forest, at Higham's Park near Chingford, then a somewhat desolate spot before suburbia sprang up around it. In May 1921, the body of 54-year-old George Grimshaw, a known peeping-tom, was found there. He had been hit on the head repeatedly with a heavy object and robbed. At first the motive seemed an obvious case of revenge but then police learned that shortly before his death, Grimshaw had been seen in the woods with a young woman. The mystery woman turned out to be Elsie Yeldham who had married William Yeldham just three days after the murder. It transpired that the real motive was theft; Elsie had lured Grimshaw into the woods where her fiancé killed him and robbed him. Both newly-weds were convicted and sentenced to death. William Yeldham was hanged but Elsie Yeldham was reprieved.

Ilford: Kensington Gardens

Set between The Drive and Ilford Golf Course, quiet Kensington Gardens was the unlikely setting for one of this century's great crimes of passion – the case of Thompson and Bywaters. Edith Thompson, book-keeper for a London milliner, had been married to shipping clerk Percy Thompson for six mundane years. Then, in the summer of 1921, while holidaying on the Isle of Wight, Edith struck up a friendship with Frederick Bywaters, a young ship's writer eight years her junior, and the two became lovers. Around midnight on 3 October 1922, the Thompsons were walking along deserted Kensington Gardens to their home at No.41

after catching the train back from a night out at the theatre in London when footsteps approached from behind. Following a brief altercation, Percy Thompson was fatally stabbed. The killer was Bywaters who had been lying in wait for their return. Letters written by Edith to Bywaters were discovered in which she strongly hinted at doing away with her husband. It was even suggested that she had arranged for the murder to take place that very night. Edith was charged with inciting Bywaters to murder and the pair stood in the dock together at the Old Bailey. At the end of a sensational trial, both were found guilty and sentenced to death. Appropriately, the two lovers were executed at the same hour on the same day, 9 January 1923, Bywaters at Pentonville Prison and Edith Thompson at Holloway.

Leigh-on-Sea: Cranham, Undercliff Gardens

On 6 June 1945, the 17-year-old daughter of Frederick and Cissie Lucas arrived home from work to find her parents had been bludgeoned to death. Mr Lucas was a jeweller and the family lived in a house in Undercliff Gardens, Leigh-on-Sea, a few miles west of Southend. The couple had received a number of savage blows to the head. Mr Lucas died shortly afterwards but his wife survived for another seven hours although she was dead by the time her daughter came home. The murderer was John Riley Young who began by attacking the couple with the leg of a stool but used such force that the leg broke and he had to resort to a flat board. When arrested, Young tried to slash his wrists. He was executed at Pentonville Prison.

Rayleigh

The Rayleigh Bath-Chair Murder was a curious affair, a desperate case of patricide that was achieved by a most unusual device. The victim was 47-year-old Archibald Brown who lived with his wife and two sons at Summerfield, London Road, Rayleigh. Although confined to a wheelchair, he still ruled the family with a rod of iron, most of his fury being aimed at his eldest son, 19-year-old bank clerk Eric. On 23 July 1943, Mr Brown was taken for his usual afternoon walk by Nurse Mitchell. They had gone about a mile when there was an almighty explosion. Nurse Mitchell emerged unscathed but Mr Brown was blown clean away. Investigations showed that the explosion had been caused by a British Hawkins No. 75 Grenade Mine, commonly used in anti-tank warfare, which had been placed beneath the velveteen cushion of the wheelchair. Eric Brown, who was serving in the army at the time, confessed, saying: 'My father is now out of his suffering, and I earnestly hope that my mother will now have a much happier and normal life.' Eric was found guilty but insane.

Stapleford Abbotts

Ex-convicts Frederick Guy Browne and William Henry Kennedy set off from their homes in London to burgle a house and steal a car in Billericay on the night of 27 September 1927. The burglary was unsuccessful but they did manage to steal the car belonging to a local physician, Dr Lovell. Ten miles away, PC Gutteridge was patrolling a lonely lane at Howe Green near Stapleford Abbotts between Abridge and Ongar when he encountered Browne and Kennedy making a speedy getaway.

He challenged the car which he recognised as Dr Lovell's vehicle, but was alerted to something suspicious when he saw that neither occupant was the good doctor. As PC Gutteridge produced his notebook, he was shot and fell staggering to the grass verge. While he lay there, two more bullets deliberately put out his eyes. The nation was horrified at this callous and totally unnecessary act but no real progress in catching the perpetrators was made for four months. Then Browne was arrested in Clapham for stealing a car. In Browne's garage police found a Webley revolver which ballistics expert Robert Churchill was later able to prove killed PC Gutteridge. Kennedy was quickly detained in Liverpool and both were convicted of murder and executed.

Tolleshunt D'Arcy: White House Farm

At 3.36 on the morning of 7 August 1985, 25-year-old Jeremy Bamber phoned Chelmsford police to say that his sister had rum amok with a gun at White House Farm in the tiny village of Tolleshunt D'Arcy, six miles northeast of Maldon. Inside the 18th-century farmhouse, police found five members of the Bamber family shot dead, including the six-year-old twin sons of Jeremy's sister, former model Sheila 'Bambi' Caffell. With her history of mental instability, the evidence did suggest that Sheila was the culprit. But the real killer was Jeremy Bamber who hated his adopted family and was desperate to lay his hands on their £500,000 inheritance. Bamber lived in a converted farm cottage at Goldhanger, three miles west of White House farm. It emerged that on the night of the slaughter he had cycled to White House Farm and had broken in through the lavatory window when everyone had gone to bed. He then unlocked his father's gun cabinet and removed a German automatic rifle with a silencer. As he was screwing on the silencer, it is believed he was confronted by Nevill Bamber in the kitchen. Jeremy Bamber shot him, battered him to the floor with the gun butt and then fired four more shots into his head. Having reloaded, Bamber went upstairs and shot his mother. Then he went to Sheila's room, put the muzzle under her chin as she slept and pulled the trigger to make it look like suicide. Meanwhile Mrs Bamber had managed to crawl to the doorway of Sheila's room where Bamber finished her off. To complete the carnage, Bamber shot his two nephews as they slept in their beds. His night's work complete, Bamber returned home and a couple of hours later, phoned the police. But his carefree behaviour in the wake of such tragedy disturbed his girlfriend who passed on her fears to the police. Brought to trial and found guilty of murder, Jeremy Bamber received five life sentences.

HERTFORDSHIRE

Aldenham: Gills Hill Lane

William Weare, John Thurtell, Joseph Hunt and William Probert were a quartet of common ruffians. So it was entirely in character that when Weare won some money from Thurtell over a game of billiards, Thurtell decided to kill him. In September 1823, Weare and the others were invited for a shooting weekend at Probert's cottage in Gills Hill Lane near Aldenham, between Radlett and Watford. Weare and Thurtell travelled in the same gig and as they approached the cottage, Thurtell pulled a gun and shot Weare in the face, the bullet glancing off his cheek-bone. The petrified Weare jumped from the gig and ran along the lane, pleading for mercy, even offering to repay the money he had won. But Thurtell refused to be denied his pleasure and over-powered Weare, slitting his throat with a penknife. For good measure, Thurtell rammed the pistol into Weare's head with such force that the barrell was filled with blood and brain tissue. The body was then dumped into the pond in Probert's garden before being moved to another pond nearby. Thurtell and Hunt tried to cover up evidence of a murder by retrieving the gun and knife but they searched the wrong part of the hedgerow and it was left to a group of labourers to find the weapons and report the matter to the police. Probert then turned King's evidence and the bloodthirsty Thurtell was hanged.

Bovingdon: John Hadland's Ltd

Employees at Hadland's, a photographic engineering firm in Bovingdon, were puzzled by the spate of illness which had struck down 70 members of the workforce in 1971. They christened it 'The Bovingdon Bug'. They thought it was probably a result of the contaminated water but certainly would not have suspected that it was really a product of the contaminated mind of mass poisoner Graham Young. Released from Broadmoor after poisoning a school friend and members of his own family, 23-year-old Young joined Hadland's on 10 May 1971 as a storekeeper. He immediately set to work, buying quantities of thallium in London, storing it at his rented room in Maynard's Road, Hemel Hempstead, and slipping it into the tea of his unsuspecting colleagues. Young's first victim was 59-year-old stores supervisor Bob Egle, chosen for no other reason than that Young worked closely with him and could therefore observe the effects of varying doses of thallium. Bob Egle was taken ill within a month of Young's arrival, reporting severe stomach pains and diarrhoea. Naturally, he recovered a little while on holiday at Great Yarmouth but a couple of days before he was due to return to work, Young bought 25 grains of thallium, giving the name of M. E. Evans and an address in Willesden, just as he had in his days as a boy poisoner. The day after he came back to Hadland's, Bob Egle was taken ill again. His fingers became numb and soon his whole body was paralysed. He died on 7 July. Another employee, Fred Biggs, also died before Young was finally arrested and sentenced to life imprisonment. 'The Bovingdon Bug' had been cured at last.

Leverstock Green: Green Lane

Diane Setty liked to visit the lay-by cafés on the A5 between Redbourne and Markyate. One afternoon in 1956, she was picked up by a middle-aged man of Mediterranean appearance in the Crow's Nest Café. They left about 2.30 pm and were seen 20 minutes later, apparently embracing in the back of a car, by two schoolboys cycling along Green Lane, near Leverstock Green on the eastern fringe of Hemel Hempstead. A few minutes later, another witness saw the car driving away from Green Lane. She remembered that the girl's face was 'twisted' which suggests she was probably dead by then. Diane's body was thrown in a ditch at Leverstock Green from a car just after 3pm. She had been strangled with a scarf. Two more boys actually saw a man dump the girl's body, cover it with her coat and drive off, yet he has never been caught. One of the boys even took what he thought was the car registration number ... but it turned out to be a three-wheeled milk float.

Potters Bar Golf Course

Foul play has twice taken place on the hallowed turf of Potters Bar Golf Course. The first time was on 18 November 1947 after 44-year-old railwayman Albert Welsh had left a note for his wife at their home near the course: 'I have gone for a walk. Shan't be in for tea – Albert.' Somewhere on that walk, Albert encountered his murderer who struck him with ferocious blows to the head before dismembering the body. Albert remained a missing person until the following May when two schoolboys, in search of lost golf balls, saw a human arm protruding from the greenery surrounding a pond adjacent to the

7th green. On dragging the pond, police found various pieces of Albert's body. His killer has never been caught.

Potters Bar Golf Course

A better-known murder occurred on Potters Bar Golf Course on 28 April 1955. The victim was Mrs Elizabeth Currell who was taking her dog for an evening walk on the course, something she had done regularly for the previous four years. When the dog returned home alone, Mr Currell reported his wife missing. The next morning, her body was found in the rough near the 17th tee. A stocking was tied around her throat but the cause of death had been a blow from a heavy iron tee-marker lying nearby, which gave a bloody palm print. No fewer than 9,000 palm prints were taken from local residents and eventually on 19 August, one matched that on the tee-marker. It belonged to 17-year-old Michael Queripel, a clerk with Potters Bar Urban District Council. He said he had been walking on the course in an attempt to get rid of a migraine when he spotted a woman walking her dog. 'I waited 'til she was out of sight behind the trees. I walked over to the green and waited.' He then attacked Mrs Currell, hitting her on the jaw, and tried to strangle her with the stocking. As she struggled, he hit her with a piece of wood but that broke so he resorted to the tee-marker which killed her. He then rushed home and cut his arm with a razor blade to explain away the blood on his clothing. But the powers of fingerprinting caught up with Queripel. He pleaded guilty to murder and was ordered to be detained at Her Majesty's pleasure.

Stocking Pelham: Rooks Farm

A few miles west of that other famous murder farm, Moat Farm, lies Rook Farm in the village of Stocking Pelham on the border of Hertfordshire and Essex. It hit the headlines in 1970 when what started out as a bungled kidnapping ended in a tragic murder. A run-down 17th century farmhouse standing in 11 acres of land, Rooks Farm was home to brothers Arthur and Nizamodeen Hosein. Desperate for money, they planned to kidnap the young wife of newspaper tycoon Rupert Murdoch but followed the company Rolls-Royce at a time when Murdoch was out of the country. It led them to St Mary House, 20 Arthur Road, Wimbledon, where by mistake, on 29 December 1969, they seized 55-year-old Mrs Muriel McKay, wife of Murdoch executive Alick McKay. Following a succession of phone calls and ransom demands, a car seen near a pick-up point was traced to Arthur Hosein. He and his brother were arrested and sentenced to life for murder. St Mary House and Rooks Farm were both sold but the body of Muriel McKay was never recovered. It is believed she was murdered at Rooks Farm and her dismembered body fed to the pigs.

Nr Wheathampstead: Nomansland Common

In a hollow on Nomansland Common less than 50 yards from the B651 Wheathampstead – St. Albans road, two children stumbled across the body of missing Australian heiress Janie Shepherd on 18 April 1977. Janie, 24, had not been seen since the evening of Friday 4 February 1977 when she had left her St John's Wood flat in a dark blue Mini Cooper, intending to spend the weekend with her boyfriend in Chelsea. She stopped at the Europa

Supermarket in Queensway but never made it to Chelsea. Her car was found four days later parked in Elgin Crescent, Notting Hill, with two deep slashes in the sun roof. Even after Janie's body had been found, no one stood trial for her murder for another 13 years. Then David Lashley, who was serving 15 years for attempted murder, boasted to a fellow prisoner that he had killed Janie. It emerged that he had threatened her with a knife in her car and made her drive to a quiet part of Ladbroke Grove where he had raped her and murdered her by crushing her throat with his fist. Janie's clothes had been badly torn in the knife attack and so Lashley took one of her spare sweaters, put it on her and strapped the corpse into the passenger seat for the drive to Nomansland Common. The prisoner to whom Lashley confessed said: 'He thought it was funny because when he went round a corner or a bend in the road, the body would sway from side to side.' Lashley was sentenced to life imprisonment in 1990.

OXFORDSHIRE

Nr Burford

Down the centuries, murder has been committed for all manner of financial gain – cash, jewellery, even furniture. But surely a 1931 case from Oxfordshire is the only known instance of someone being murdered for their cycle lamp! On 19 December of that year, two cyclists came across the body of Mrs Mabel Matthews lying next to her bicycle at the side of the Oxford-Cheltenham road near Burford. She had been battered around the head, kicked and partially strangled. Missing were her groceries and her acetylene cycle lamp. Found near the scene of the crime was a duffle bag, containing sausage sandwiches. The bag was traced to a soldier, Private G. T. Pople, and from his lips came the bizarre motive for Mrs Matthews' murder. Bored with his electric cycle lamp, Pople had set his heart on an acetlyene model and when he saw Mrs Matthews cycling along the road with the very lamp he coveted, he made a grab for it as she rode past. He claimed that his trousers caught in the pedal of his own bicycle and in the resulting melee, he and Mrs Matthews rolled down the slope. There, he said, he found her unconscious. Pople then stole her lamp and groceries before casting aside his unwanted electric lamp further along the road. But the jury didn't believe Pople's claim that it was an accident. He was found guilty and hanged for killing the lady with the lamp.

Nr Charlbury: Shear's Copse, Ditchley Park

The night of 19 December 1861 sported a full moon – a poacher's moon – ideal for the illegal activities of John Hall and John Tuckey. The pair had been drinking that evening at two hostelries in Charlbury, the Oxford House and the Royal Oak, before collecting a repaired rifle from Hall's brother-in-law and setting off for a night of poaching on Lord Dillon's estate at nearby Ditchley Park. Stephen Moulder, a father of seven children, was guarding his Lordship's pheasants with the help of another gamekeeper. Around 1.30 am, they tackled Hall and Tuckey in Shear's Copse and Hall shot Moulder dead. Hall, a 33-year-old former soldier, was found guilty of murder but the jury recommended mercy and his death sentence was commuted to penal servitude for life.

Fulbrook

Six years after the cycle lamp murder, another tragedy hit the Burford area when 17-month-old Kathleen Woodward was found strangled by the side of the road in the village of Fulbrook, a mile to the north of Burford en route to Chipping Norton. She had been strangled with a section of clothes-line. The infant's killer was 25-year-old John Edward Allen, assistant chef of the Lamb Hotel in Burford. Allen had become friendly with Kathleen's parents, Mr and Mrs Frederick Woodward, who also worked at the hotel. Allen regularly played with the little girl, taking her for rides on his bicycle. When he took her out on 19 June 1937, Mrs Woodward's parting words were: 'Be careful, John, don't hurt her.' Kathleen's body was found later that day and Allen fled to

London where he later gave himself up. At the trial, Mrs Woodward stated that the motive for the murder was jealousy because she and not Allen had been placed in charge of making the cakes for a forthcoming banquet at the hotel. Allen, who had twice previously been in mental institutions, was committed to Broadmoor.

Gallowstree Common: The Crown and Anchor Inn

The Crown and Anchor Inn, near Kidmore End, about five miles north of Reading, was owned by 55-year-old widow Sarah Blake. On the morning of 4 March 1922, she was found dead on the kitchen floor, the result of a severe beating with an iron bar coupled with a frenzied knife attack. She had sustained a fractured skull and in total there were over 60 bruises and wounds on her body. The last guest to see her alive the previous evening was 15-year-old Jack Hewett who lived nearby with his mother and stepfather. A knife found in a hedge near the inn was recognised as Hewett's by the foreman at Paddocks Farm where the lad worked. Human blood-stains were discovered on Hewett's jacket. He initially confessed but later changed his mind. The jury were more certain and Hewett was found guilty and sentenced to be detained indefinitely. No real motive was ever established although it has been suggested that Hewett committed the dreadful deed after watching a disturbing scene at the cinema.

Henley-on-Thames

Lawyer Francis Blandy lived in a sizeable house beside the river at Henley with his wife and daughter Mary. Mr Blandy was keen to find Mary a husband and offered a handsome dowry of £10,000 to a suitable suitor. The ideal candidate seemed to present himself in the shape of army captain the Hon. William Cranstoun, who at 46 was 20 years older than Mary. He seemed delighted to have gained Mary's hand but soon the Blandys learned that Cranstoun already had a wife in Scotland – not to mention a baby. Cranstoun tried in vain to prove that the marriage was not real but Mr Blandy was no longer interested in him as a prospective son-in-law, particularly since he showed a little too much interest in the dowry. Yet Mary was still in love with Cranstoun and they bemoaned the fact that her father was preventing their relationship from blossoming. One day Cranstoun sent Mary a powder which he said was a love philtre obtained from an old Highland witch. Cranstoun suggested that if Mary were to slip the powder into her father's tea, it might persuade him to look more favourably on Cranstoun. So Mary did as her lover bade with the result that Mr Blandy quickly died on 14 August 1751 of arsenic poisoning. The not-so-honourable Cranstoun fled abroad, leaving Mary to face the gallows. She was hanged outside Oxford Castle on 6 April 1752. As she mounted the ladder to the scaffold, she spotted that the beam attached to two trees, which acted as a gallows, was placed inordinately high. Like all 18th century ladies, she wore no drawers and didn't relish the prospect of local ruffians peering up at her in her state of inertia. So she pleaded with her executioners: 'For decency's sake, gentlemen, don't hang me high!'

Nr Nettlebed: Rumerhedge Wood

A lonely spot in dark, sinister Rumerhedge Wood formed the backdrop for the final act in a deadly passion play. Draughtsman Raymond Cook was married to strong-minded school-teacher June while pursuing an affair with the dangerously manipulative Valerie 'Kim' Newall. In a bid to repair the rift in their marriage, Mrs Cook altered her will to make her husband, not their children, the main beneficiary. Meanwhile Newall was pregnant by Cook and demanding money. She persuaded her lover that the only way he could afford to keep her was to ensure that Mrs Cook died while the will was in his favour. Newall planned to make Mrs Cook's murder look like an accident, even pinpointing the precise beech tree in Rumerhedge Wood (near Hook End, south of Nettlebed) which the Cooks' car was to hit. Newall also recruited a friend, Eric Jones, blackmailing him into helping after he had performed an abortion on her. Her plot was hatched on the evening of 2 March 1967. The Cooks went out to dinner at the George Hotel in Pangbourne, returning to their home in Reading by the scenic route. Jones was waiting on the narrow, winding lane through Rumerhedge Wood and as the Cooks' red Mini passed at the appointed time of 9.30 pm, he flagged them down, pretending he had a flat tyre. Cook, who was in the passenger seat, offered Jones a lift and once inside the Mini, the pair of them attacked Mrs Cook, initially with fists and then with a car jack. They then drove the car into the tree. The police arrived at the scene of the 'accident' to find Mrs Cook unconscious (she died shortly afterwards) and Cook apparently dazed. But the master plan failed because there was insufficient damage to the exterior of the car to justify the amount of blood within: Forensic evidence later revealed that the car had only been travelling at 10 mph when it struck the tree! Cook, Jones and Newall were found guilty of murder and sentenced to life imprisonment.

Oxford: Wycliffe Hall

Quiet, bespectacled John Stanley Phillips, son of a Woking vicar, and an earnest theological student at Wycliffe Hall, Oxford, seemed just about the least likely person to commit murder. However, 21-year-old Phillips was a seething mass of abnormal fantasies and was dangerously obsessed with religion and sex. On 5 February 1938 the butler of Wycliffe Hall realised that 16-year-old pantry boy Harold Matthews was missing. The Hall was combed from top to bottom but it was not until the next day, when the search took in the roof, that Harold's body was found, naked and hideously mutilated. The trail led to Phillips' room. A pool of blood was found beneath his carpet and his trousers were bloodstained too. Young Harold had been bound and strangled before the body was hidden in a trunk. Phillips was found guilty of the crime but insane.

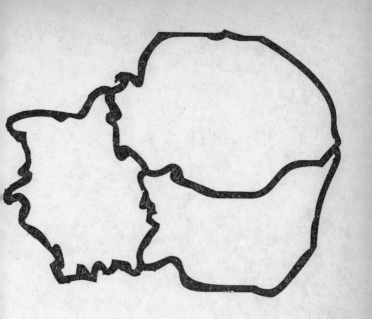

EAST
ANGLIA

CAMBRIDGESHIRE

Ailsworth: 2a Maffit Road

The village of Ailsworth, four miles west of Peterborough, is hardly the sort of location where one expects to encounter contract killers. Yet when 51-year-old former beauty queen Muriel McCullough decided she had tired of marriage to her wealthy second husband Bill, she hired a hitman from her home town of Liverpool in what became known as the 'Kiss of Death' case. She paid merchant seaman James Collingwood £8,000 to kill her husband. On the evening of 17 November 1981, Muriel McCullough had made sure she was well away from Ailsworth and was staying at a house in Liverpool. She phoned her home, ostensibly to wish a loving goodnight to her husband from whom she was temporarily parted, but in reality to check that he was alone. Reassured that he was, she gave Collingwood the go-ahead and Bill McCullough was shot twice in the head while he lay asleep. Collingwood's accomplice, Alan Kay, waited outside the house and then drove the hitman to London in Bill McCullough's car. But Muriel McCullough was unable to get away with murder and she, Collingwood and Kay were each jailed for life.

Nr Buckden

One of the most baffling cases of the 1980s was the discovery of the body of 36-year-old solicitor Janice Weston in a northbound lay-by on the A1 near Buckden, just south of Huntingdon. Janice Weston was a partner in a Lincoln's Inn firm and had left work shortly after 5 pm on Saturday 10 September 1983 for the Holland Park flat which she shared with her husband Tony. At the time, he was away in France on business. She appeared to have left the flat hurriedly before driving off in her silver Alfa Romeo. Her battered body was found by a cyclist, who had stopped to answer nature's call, in a ditch alongside the lay-by, just 15 miles from the couple's country retreat, Clopton Manor in Northamptonshire. She had been killed that night with a car jack, found in a nearby field. The killer had made off in her car which was later found parked in Camden Square, London NW1. The interior was smeared with blood. Yet although the lay-by was completely exposed to the traffic on the busy A1, there were few witnesses and Janice Weston's murder remains unsolved.

Ely

Sixteen-year-old Amy Hutchinson paid the ultimate penalty for marrying on the rebound. Amy, who hailed from Whittlesey, was overcome with grief when the love of her life left to seek his fame and fortune in London. So she accepted the marriage offer of John Hutchinson, a sickly soul. Then out of the blue, her young man returned from London on the very day of the wedding. It was too late for Amy to cancel the nuptials so she decided to kill her husband and laced his ale with white arsenic. He died at their home in Ely on 14 October 1748. Somewhat indiscreetly, she immediately returned to her former lover and local gossip caused John Hutchinson's body to be exhumed with disastrous consequences. Found guilty of murder, Amy was strangled and burned.

Nr Newborough

Peterborough lorry driver Morris Clarke had convinced himself that his wife was having an affair with her former boss, 53-year-old farmer Arthur Johnson. Mrs Clarke had once been housekeeper to Johnson at Crowtree Farm, near Newborough, a few miles to the north of Peterborough in the heart of fenland. On 15 October 1956, after a bitter row with his wife, 27-year-old Clarke headed for Crowtree Farm. Claiming that Johnson attacked him first, Clarke hit his adversary over the head with a piece of wood, killing him. He then hid the body in a drainage dyke three miles away where it was found ten days later. Clarke had found the victim's safe key in his pocket during the incident and emptied it of £700 before he left. Found guilty of murder, Clarke was sentenced to death but earned a reprieve.

Whittlesey

Richard Faulkner was a deeply unpleasant youth. On 15 February 1810, at the age of 15, Faulkner beat 12-year-old George Burnham to death, merely to gain revenge on Burnham's mother who had thrown a bucket of dirty water over him. After his conviction, Faulkner was so aggressive while detained in the condemned cell that his hands and feet had to be chained to the wall. In a final attempt to calm him down, the authorities decided to introduce into the cell a boy who looked uncannily like the deceased. Suddenly, Faulkner became meek and mild, confessed to the murder and begged forgiveness. It may have eased his mind but it did little for his body since he was executed the following Monday.

NORFOLK

Catton, nr Norwich

Young lovers Dennis Moore and Eileen Cullen were just two weeks away from their wedding when a silly argument led to murder. On the day of the murder in 1951, the couple had been to the doctor to ensure that Eileen's pregnancy was progressing satisfactorily and had then gone shopping for her wedding outfit. Returning to their home in Catton, a village on the northern outskirts of Norwich, they decided to go for a walk. In the course of their perambulation, a row developed when Eileen refused to have sex and Moore strangled her in a cowshed. Moore himself led detectives to the cowshed and before they could intervene, he ran in and threw himself across the body crying: 'I love you. I love you.' For all his penitence, 22-year-old Dennis Moore was hanged.

Cockley Cley, Swaffham Forest

Engulfing parts of the A1065 between Swaffham and Brandon is Swaffham Forest, an ideal hideout with its mixture of dense woodland and a tangled web of bracken. At dawn on 27 August 1974, a farmer and his son were walking down a farm track leading off the main road near Cockley Cley when they came across a parcel with a human foot sticking out. It had been buried in the bracken but had been disturbed by foxes in search of food. The contents revealed the headless corpse of a woman in her mid 20s wearing a pink Marks & Spencer nightie. The body was wrapped in a National Cash Register plastic dust sheet. All clues had been carefully removed – the nightdress was one of 112,000 of that size sold throughout the UK – and the body was unidentifiable. But for the foxes, it may never have been found.

East Dereham

In 1951, the ancient market town of East Dereham, 15 miles west of Norwich, was the setting for a lover's death that the murderer tried to pass off as a suicide pact. On learning that his 19-year-old girlfriend Ellen Ludkin was pregnant, Alfred Reynolds, 24, had wanted to make an honest woman of her. But the girl's father forbade the marriage. According to Reynolds, he went round to her house in Dereham when her father was out and they walked to a nearby cycle shed. There, Reynolds said, he told her he was going to shoot himself. Reynolds stated that Ellen reacted to his news by pleading: 'Shoot me first – you can't leave me in this world all alone. Let's go together.' Reynolds said he loaded the gun and pointed it at his head but before he could pull the trigger, she turned the gun towards her own face and begged: 'Shoot me first.' He said her parting words were: 'Goodbye darling. Keep your promise.' And then she shot herself dead. But Reynolds was charged with murder and the prosecution was able to prove that the distance between the end of the gun and the trigger was too great for Ellen to have fired the fatal bullet. Why was it also that Reynolds had not kept his end of the bargain? He reasoned that he hadn't shot himself because he wanted people to know why they had made the pact. The jury were not convinced and subsequently found Reynolds guilty of murder. The anguished lover was hanged.

Great Yarmouth: South Beach

Although married, Herbert and Mary Bennett led separate lives. He worked as a labourer at Woolwich Arsenal yet rarely visited his wife who lived in Bexleyheath. Thus when he met parlourmaid Alice Meadows, 20-year-old Bennett was able to convince her that he was single and they became engaged. But Bennett realised his duplicity would be found out eventually and so he determined to murder his wife. Mrs Bennett wanted a summer holiday and her husband suggested she take a break in Great Yarmouth. He would even come and meet her there. They arranged to meet on the night of Saturday 22 September 1900 outside the Town Hall. Having put her child to bed, Mrs Bennett left her lodgings and set off for the rendezvous. Bennett took her for a drink and then they headed towards the South Beach where the dunes and hollows were frequented by countless courting couples. They snuggled down in one such hollow and Mrs Bennett, who still loved him, suspected nothing. As they embraced, Bennett quietly pulled a nine-inch, mohair boot-lace from his pocket, twisted it around her neck and tied it into a knot, slowly throttling her. Nearby couples who heard a woman's voice pleading for mercy thought it was just high jinks. A gold chain found in Bennett's possession linked him to the murder scene and he was hanged at Norwich on 21 March 1901.

Great Yarmouth: South Beach

Twelve years after Mary Bennett's murder, another woman's body was found on almost precisely the same spot on South Beach and she too had been strangled with a bootlace, this time taken from one of her own shoes. The major difference between the two cases was that it seems the second murder was committed elsewhere and the body then taken to the beach. It was that of 18-year-old Dora Grey who lived near the cattle-market and worked in a boarding house in Manby Road. On 14 July 1912, she told a friend that she had been to Lowestoft with a 'gentleman' and was going to meet him again that evening. She was last seen alive walking towards the South Beach. Her killer was never traced.

Great Yarmouth: Owles Court

Norman Goldthorpe was down on his luck. His wife had left him to elope with a soldier and his present lover was contemplating returning to her husband in Yorkshire. In an effort to drown his sorrows he turned to the bottle. The more he drank, the more jealous he became until one Friday evening in August 1950, he decided to exact revenge by finding a woman of his own. His choice was a 66-year-old prostitute named Emma Howe who frequented the Great Eastern public house. When the stocky Goldthorpe lurched into the establishment, Emma had gone home after what was clearly not one of her more profitable evenings. He found that she lived in a tiny one-roomed house at Owles Court which was then considered a disreputable part of town. When he called round, they went to bed where he strangled her. He attempted to creep out in the early hours but was spotted by a neighbour and arrested the following afternoon in the Great Eastern, still somewhat the worse for wear. He was hanged at Norwich.

Norwich: St Martins-at-Plow

During a drunken quarrel at their home in St Martins-at-Plow, Norwich, in June 1851, tailor William Sheward stabbed his wife Martha to death with a pair of his working shears. He then set about dismembering the body, boiling pieces in a saucepan and distributing them around the Thorpe area of the city. He emptied the entrails in Bishopsgate Street while his wife's long hair, which he had cut into pieces, blew away as he walked along. First to be found was a hand in Lakenham Lane, about a mile and a half from Sheward's home, on 21 June, and soon a wool-stapler from Trowse reported that his dog had brought in a foot. The recovered portions were preserved in spirits at Norwich's Guildhall. Yet, although a human jigsaw was slowly being assembled, the victim was not positively identified and Sheward remained free. He remarried in 1862 and six years later became landlord of the Key and Castle Sun at Norwich. Finally in 1869, drunk and plagued by his conscience, Sheward admitted having murdered his wife, adding that she was still partly pickled in the Guildhall. When he sobered up, he tried to retract his confession but was found guilty and hanged.

Sculthorpe: U.S. Air Force base

Tall and athletic in his late thirties, U.S. Air Force Master Sergeant Marcus Marymont was very much the extrovert party-goer. But his marriage to Mary Helen, six years his senior, was going through a rocky patch and didn't improve when in 1956 Marymont was posted to the base at Sculthorpe, just west of Fakenham. On a visit to a nightclub in Maidenhead, which had a reputation for welcoming U.S. servicemen, he met a kindred spirit in vivacious Cynthia Taylor who was 22 and separated from her husband. Marymont admitted that he was married but told Cynthia that his wife and three children were living in the States. Their affair flourished but Marymont knew that if it was to continue, he would have to do away with his wife. On 9 June 1958, Mary Helen attended a luncheon at King's Lynn after which she collapsed in agony with chronic diarrhoea. She died in hospital a few days later. Since nobody else at the lunch had fallen ill, food poisoning was ruled out and despite Marymont's objections, a post-mortem was ordered. Arsenic was found in her body and two cleaners at the base remembered Marymont asking them where he could obtain arsenic. Tried by a U.S. General Court Martial at Denham, Marymont was found guilty of murder and sentenced to life imprisonment, to be served at Fort Leavenworth Prison, Kansas.

Tilney St Lawrence

Between King's Lynn and Wisbech sits a gaggle of villages with names such as Terrington St Clement, Walpole St Andrew and Wiggenhall St Mary Magdalen. Among them, just off the main A47, is Tilney St Lawrence where, in the early part of the century, Wallace Benton ran a small fruit farm. By 1929, he was 70, shortsighted and virtually stone deaf. Not surprisingly the business had been allowed to slide dramatically. The property was put up for auction and an order of ejection was made against Benton. Thomas Williamson, who lived nearby, was chosen to try and repair the years of Benton neglect. Benton was furious and on the evening of 21 March 1929, the day before the order of ejection was to be enforced, he fetched his shotgun and killed Williamson in a nearby stable. Benton claimed it was an accident but, at the end of a trial in which everything had to be repeated at least once for the deaf defendant, he was found guilty of murder. However the death sentence was commuted.

Wymondham: Stanfield Hall

Auctioneer James Blomfield Rush was a tenant farmer on the large Stanfield Hall estate, just to the east of Wymondham. Rush's landlord was the distinguished Isaac Jermy, a barrister and the Recorder of Norwich, and it was from Jermy that Rush had borrowed £5,000 to buy Potash Farm. Jermy soon regretted the loan for not only did Rush seduce the Jermys' governess, Emily Sandford, but he was forced to take Rush to court to recover the money he was owed. The £5,000 was due for repayment on 30 November 1848. On the foggy night of the 28th just after 8 pm, the Jermy family were sitting in the drawing-room of Stanfield Hall after dinner. Isaac heard a strange sound and went to the front door to investigate. A shot rang out and the old man was killed. His son, Jermy Jermy, followed and was confronted by a figure holding two pistols and wearing a voluminous cloak and a red and black mask. Jermy Jermy was also fatally shot. The bloodshed continued and Jermy Jermy's wife and the maid, Eliza Chestney, were both seriously wounded while the butler hid in the pantry.

The killer fled but was soon identified as Rush. He was hanged outside Norwich Prison on 23 April 1849.

SUFFOLK

Cowlinge: Branches Park

Six miles south-east of Newmarket is the estate of Branches Park, home in 1956 to wealthy 71-year-old eccentric Rachel Parsons. In Miss Parsons' case, eccentric was often a euphemism for bad-tempered since she had the reputation of treating her beloved racehorses considerably better than her staff. On 1 July, one of her stablemen made a routine request for his holiday money. She flatly refused to pay him and attacked him with her handbag. The only way he could get her to stop was to hit her with an iron bar, a blow which proved to be fatal. Then he stole Miss Parsons' binoculars and sold them. When police questioned him about the transaction, the stableman confessed to the killing. At his trial, the jury decided he had acted under great provocation and the murder charge was reduced to one of manslaughter. He was sent to prison for ten years.

Peasenhall: Providence House

A violent thunderstorm struck the Suffolk countryside on the night of 31 May 1902, causing considerable consternation in the village of Peasenhall, some 20 miles to the north of Ipswich. Residents came to their doors to gaze at the mighty flashes of lightning. Meanwhile, a minute's walk away from the centre of the village at 17th century Providence House, home of Deacon Crisp and his family, the household was stirred by a loud crash and a scream. Possibly attributing it to the storm, nobody paid any undue attention until next morning when William Harsent, father of the Crisps' 23-year-old maid Rose, arrived at Providence House with her weekly supply of clean linen. He let himself in through the back door to the kitchen and prepared to climb the stairs to the attic which served as her quarters. But to his horror at the foot of the stairs, he found his daughter lying dead with her throat cut. Her nightdress was badly charred from what would appear to have been an attempt by her killer to burn the corpse. Near Rose's body was a medicine bottle, the label of which indicated that the contents had been prescribed for the children of 34-year-old William Gardiner, a Methodist Elder and foreman at a local agricultural factory. He immediately emerged as the main suspect because villagers believed that he had been conducting an illicit affair with Rose Harsent while the post-mortem revealed that Rose was six months pregnant. Gardiner was charged with murder but was twice acquitted. The Peasenhall Mystery remains unsolved, but village legend has it that the troubled soul of Rose Harsent causes a violent storm over the village once every seven years.

Polstead: The Red Barn, off Marten's Lane

The Red Barn Murder at Polstead, eight miles east of Sudbury, was one of the most famous 19th century crimes, inspiring songs, porcelain figures and even a London stage play. The central characters were William Corder, 21, a prosperous farmer from Polstead, and mole-catcher's daughter Maria Marten who was 25. Corder had made Maria pregnant and although the child

died, he was still put under great pressure to marry
Maria. The shameful Corder continued to prevaricate
until on 18 May 1827 he told Maria to meet him in
secrecy at the Red Barn, a red tiled building on his own
land, from where, he promised, they would travel to
Ipswich to be married the following day. Maria was
never seen alive again. For, at the barn, Corder shot her
through the head and stabbed her through the heart.
After the murder, Corder wrote to Maria's parents, saying that they had been married in London and were
living happily in the Isle of Wight. But the Martens were
suspicious, particularly as there had been no letters
from Maria herself, and Mrs Marten started to have vivid
dreams that her daughter's body lay buried in the Red
Barn. At her insistence, the police finally searched the
barn in April 1828 and found Maria's body. Meanwhile
Corder had advertised for a wife in London and had
selected and married a respectable schoolmistress from
over 45 eager candidates. It must have come as something of a blow to her newly-wedded bliss when he was
arrested for murder. At his trial, Corder claimed Maria
had committed suicide and that he had buried her body
for fear of being accused of killing her. But he was found
guilty and 10,000 people turned out to watch his execution at Bury St Edmunds on 11 August 1828. The old
Red Barn has gone but Corder's House (renamed Street
Farm), where the murderer used to live, still stands at
the foot of the hill leading to Polstead Green.

Sternfield, nr Saxmundham

Wealthy farmer John Beddingfield was 24 when he married his pretty young wife Ann and moved to a large

farm at Sternfield, a couple of miles south-east of Sax-mundham. But Ann soon tired of her husband and seduced one of the servants, handsome 19-year-old Richard Ringe. She begged Ringe to murder Bedding-field, not only offering her body but also half of her husband's estate. Accordingly, Ringe bought some poison and even had the nerve to ask the maid to stir it in her master's drink of rum and milk. This plan failed so Ringe resorted to more forceful means and one night in March 1763, he strangled John Beddingfield in bed. He then raced to his lover's room and announced excitedly: 'I have done for him!' Amazingly, the coroner's jury re-turned a verdict of natural death, deciding that Beddingfield had strangled himself in his bed sheets in the course of a nightmare! But a servant girl who had been in Ann's bed to warm it up, had also heard Ringe's triumphant statement and reported the truth to the police. As a result, Ringe and Ann Beddingfield were charged with murder. Found guilty, they were both hanged near Ipswich.

EAST
MIDLANDS

DERBYSHIRE

Baslow: Clod Hill Lane

Picturesque by day but moody by night, Clod Hill Lane crosses the bleak Derbyshire moors near the village of Baslow, eight miles west of Chesterfield. In the early 1960s, it was the scene for two killings of homosexuals which became known as The Carbon Copy Murders. The first victim was 60-year-old William Elliott whose body was found in the lane on 13 June 1960 with severe head injuries. Then on 29 March 1961, on the exact same stretch of road, 48-year-old Chesterfield chemist George Stobbs was found kicked to death. The police were quick to link the two murders. Both victims frequented the Spread Eagle public house in Chesterfield and in each case their cars had been abandoned in Park Road, Chesterfield. Their killer was 26-year-old former soldier Michael Copeland who had a pathological hatred for homosexuals. He was found guilty of the two murders and also that of a young soldier who had been murdered in Germany in November 1960. Copeland was sentenced to death but this was commuted to life imprisonment when it was proved that he was under mental stress at the time of the murders.

Chaddesden, nr Derby

Railway guard Percy Atkins decided that the only way to solve his tangled love life was to bury his wife on his allotment at Chaddesden on the outskirts of Derby. Atkins, 33, had been married for eight years. He and his wife lived at Francis Street in Derby but Mrs Atkins had recently been residing with her parents at Buckden in what was then Huntingdonshire. In her absence, Atkins had seized the opportunity to marry bigamously one Margaret Milton of Co-operative Street, Derby. When Atkins' wife returned to the marital home to collect one of the children, the couple went for a walk on 21 November 1921 to discuss their problems. Harmony was not restored and a quarrel ended with her throwing her wedding ring at him and storming off. According to Atkins, as he searched for the ring, he found his wife dead on a pile of boulders. Then being afraid, he said he buried the body on his allotment in a hole which he had dug for an apple tree. But his story failed to convince the jury and he was found guilty of murder and hanged.

Clay Mills

When, on the morning of 30 April 1947, a policeman opened the door of a blue Austin saloon parked on the main A38 Burton-Derby road, a few hundred yards from the canal bridge at Clay Mills, he found the body of a man slumped on the floor. The car was a Birmingham taxi and George Tyler, the owner, had been shot through the head. Late the previous evening, a nervous young man in RAF uniform had stepped into Tyler's cab at the taxi rank outside Birmingham New Street station. The car headed towards Derby but the airman has never been traced. It is believed that after the killing he doubled back to Burton and caught a train to Derby. The gun was found in a ditch at Clay Mills and Tyler's personal papers were discovered near Rolleston.

Shortly before the policeman made his fatal find, a bread delivery man, seeing the car parked with its lights on, had reached into the vehicle and switched them off. He failed to spot the body because he hadn't looked down at the floor.

Derby: 10 Walter Street

Cvijo Cvijetic, a 37-year-old Yugoslav labourer, was wrongly convinced that his German wife of only five months was having an affair with their lodger, another Yugoslav, Dane Glumac, aged 50. Cvijetic had earlier sought police advice about the situation but on 19 September 1954, he took the matter into his own hands and brutally stabbed Glumac 29 times at their home in Walter Street, Derby. After the murder, Cvijetic went straight to the police and confessed. He was found guilty but insane.

Eastmoor: Pottery Cottage

Not far from stately Chatsworth House sits Pottery Cottage (since renamed Northend Farm) on Eastmoor, the scene of one of the most horrific murder cases of the 1970s, in which three generations of a family were brutally killed. In mid-January 1977, 30-year-old prisoner William Hughes escaped from police custody on his way to Chesterfield and fled across Beeley Moor to Pottery Cottage. He terrorised the occupants for three days during which time he stabbed to death Richard Moran, his ten-year-old daughter Sarah and Mr Moran's in-laws, Arthur and Amy Minton. The sole survivor was Mr Moran's wife Gill. Finally, Hughes decided to make a run for it, armed with an axe and with Gill Moran as hostage. Following a police chase across the Peak District, Hughes' orgy of bloodshed was ended when he was shot dead by marksmen at Rainow near Macclesfield.

Simmondley Moor: Dinting Pit

Eight miles south of where Ian Brady and Myra Hindley later went about their evil business, another notorious child murderer, 62-year-old Albert Edward Burrows, killed four victims between 1920 and 1923. A farm labourer by trade, Burrows had bigamously married Hannah Calladine, who was nearly 30 years his junior, in 1918. She gave birth to a boy, also called Albert Edward, but when she discovered there was already a Mrs Burrows, she applied successfully for a bastardy order against her illegitimate 'spouse'. Unable to keep up the weekly payments of 7s, Burrows was sent to prison for 21 days. On his release, he took up residence with his real wife at Back Kershaw Street, Glossop (now demolished), but almost immediately Hannah Calladine arrived from Nantwich with her two offspring. Mrs Burrows marched out and issued a maintenance order against Burrows which was made returnable for 12 January 1920. Burrows was in a real dilemma. If he sent Hannah packing, he would have to make payments on the bastardy order; if she stayed, he would be faced with a maintenance order. Either way, he would end up back in prison since he was penniless and already behind with the rent. The only solution seemed to be to murder Hannah and her children. Hannah was last seen alive in Glossop on the evening of 11 January 1920 after which

Burrows pleaded with his wife to withdraw the maintenance summons. He told a neighbour that Hannah 'will never come to Glossop again.' It was the truest words he ever spoke. Burrows continued to live peacefully with his wife until he was questioned about the disappearance of four-year-old Thomas Wood on 4 March 1923. Burrows led the police to Dinting Pit, a drift mine on Simmondley Moor on the edge of Glossop. The boy's sexually assaulted body was found in the pit shaft and eight weeks later a further search of the shaft revealed the skeletons of Hannah Calladine and her two children, Elsie Large and Albert Edward Burrows junior. They were lying in stagnant water, over 100 feet below ground. Burrows was found guilty of murder and hanged at Nottingham on 8 August 1923.

Spondon, nr Derby

Enoch Stone, a semi-invalid of about 45, lived in poverty at Spondon, just east of Derby. His son was in service at Appleby Hall in Derby and Enoch used to make a regular round trip to collect his washing. On the night of Monday 23 June 1865, Enoch picked up the dirty laundry as usual, had a drink at the Plough Inn and walked back home via Chaddesden. Around 11.20 pm, he was brutally attacked near the Nottingham road, during which his skull was split from ear to ear. His boots were stolen and his pockets emptied for a paltry booty of 10d. Enoch died the next morning. There had been a distinct shortage of Good Samaritans that night. A passer-by heard a shout of 'murder' but decided it was just a drunk while two men stepped over Enoch dying in the road. They thought his face, blackened with blood and dirt, had been made-up as a joke. With such public-spiritedness, it was little wonder that the killer was never caught.

LEICESTERSHIRE

Leicester: 9 Sweetbriar Road

A former divisional officer with the St John Ambulance
Brigade, 75-year-old Sidney Leeson was known for his
consideration to others and sometimes offered shelter to
couples in need. On 13 September 1965, Sidney and his
son Charles were due to go on a train outing but when
his father failed to appear, Charles called round to the
house at 9 Sweetbriar Road. There he found his father in
the hall battered to death with a flower vase. He had
been killed the previous evening and £23 was found to
be missing. The murder remains unsolved, but police
were interested in a man in a duffle coat who called at a
nearby house and asked to borrow a ladder to get some
things from No. 7, the house next door to Sidney Leeson.

Leicester: Wellington Street

James Cook has a place in history as the last person in
England to be gibbeted. A 21-year-old book-binder, Cook
was heavily in debt. On 30 May 1832, John Paas, a
London engraver, called on Cook at his shop in Welling-
ton Street to collect the money he was owed. Cook
appeared to take exception to this and promptly bludgeoned Paas to death. He then dismembered the body
and burned the pieces in the shop's grate. By the following morning, smoke was billowing out. Cook told
neighbouring shopkeepers that he was burning bad dog-

meat but some were suspicious and a later analysis revealed human flesh. By then, Cook had fled to Liverpool
and was arrested while being rowed out to a ship bound
for America. He returned to face his fate and was
executed on 10 August 1832 before a crowd of 30,000.
Afterwards his body was hung for three days above the
junction of Saffron Lane and Aylestone Road.

Little Stretton: Gartree Road

The Green Bicycle Murder, one of the great unsolved
crimes of rural Britain, was an apparently motiveless
killing in a peaceful country lane six miles east of Leicester. It was on the night of 5 July 1919 that 21-year-old
Bella Wright, a rubber-factory worker, was found lying
in her own blood beside a bicycle in Gartree Rod, just
south-east of the village of Little Stretton before Burton
Overy. There was a bullet wound above her left cheek-
bone. Witnesses spoke of seeing Bella and a man on a
green bicycle on the evening of the murder. They had
ridden together to her uncle's cottage in nearby Galby
and the mystery man had waited outside for her. A green
bicycle was later dredged up from the Leicester Canal,
together with a revolver holster containing live ammunition of the type that killed Bella Wright. These items
were traced to 34-year-old Ronald Vivien Light, a Leicester man who had been invalided out of the army with
shell-shock and who now taught mathematics at Dean
Close School, Cheltenham. Charged with murder, Light
finally admitted that he owned the bicycle and that he
had met Bella on 5 July. He claimed that when he read of
Bella's fate and the search for a man with a green bicycle,
he deemed it wise to dispose of the machine as well as

his old army holster. Light convinced the jury and was found not guilty.

LINCOLNSHIRE

Kirkby on Bain: 2 Council Houses

Three miles east of Woodhall Spa nestles the sleepy Lincolnshire village of Kirkby on Bain. In 1934, there were no more than 200 residents but one of them was a fiendish murderess. She was 43-year-old gamekeeper's daughter Ethel Major who lived with her lorry driver husband Arthur at No. 2 Council Houses. They had been married for 16 years but Arthur's discovery that Ethel had an illegitimate daughter led to an understandable deterioration in their relationship. Ethel, known in the village as something of a strong willed character, began to accuse Arthur of being a drunkard and of having affairs. He responded by arranging for an advertisement to be placed in the Horncastle News in which he refused to be responsible for his wife's debts. It was to appear on 26 May 1934. Two days before, Arthur Major died. The doctor diagnosed the cause of death as epilepsy and Ethel quickly cancelled the notice in the newspaper. With even greater haste, she arranged the funeral and some mourners had already congregated at the house when the coroner stopped the proceedings. The police had received an anonymous letter saying that a neighbour's dog had died after eating scraps of food thrown out by Ethel Major. The dog's body was exhumed and found to contain strychnine. The post-mortem on Arthur Major also revealed the presence of strychnine. Ethel had poisoned his corned beef. She was found guilty of murder at Lincoln Assizes and despite the jury's recommendation for mercy, she was hanged at Hull Prison on 19 December 1934.

Wrangle

It is medically accepted that two grains of arsenic are sufficient to cause death so when 59-year-old William Leffey ate a rice pudding containing 135 grains, there was little room for doubt. Leffey and his wife Mary, 49, owned a small-holding at Wrangle, between Boston and Skegness. On 6 February 1884, Mary set off on the nine-mile journey to Boston to sell their butter. William accompanied her at first but after travelling for half an hour, he decided to walk home. By mid-afternoon, he was taken ill but managed to reach a doctor carrying a partly eaten basin of bitter rice pudding which he claimed had been poisoned. Leffey died that evening. Mary Leffey was charged with murder. The defence claimed it was suicide but Mary's case was not helped by witnesses testifying that she had once publicly wished her husband dead. Mary Leffey was found guilty and executed.

NORTHAMPTONSHIRE

Althorp

The shadows of majestic Althorp House were once witness to the dumping of a bundle made by one Andrew MacRae. Riddled with maggots, it was discovered in a ditch on the Northampton-Rugby road, half a mile from Althorp station, on 6 August 1892. The bundle contained a woman's legs and some baby clothes. The limbs were identified as the legs of Annie Pritchard who had literally been butchered by MacRae, a crime for which he was to hang. Andrew MacRae had left his wife and two children in Birmingham while he went to work in Northampton for his brother Edward, a butcher who owned a warehouse in Dyechurch Lane. Posing as a Mr Anderson (to conceal his marital status), Andrew MacRae began an affair with Annie Pritchard who soon became infatuated with her beau. Blissfully unaware of MacRae's double life, Annie had a baby in June 1892 and announced that she and 'Anderson' were to be married before sailing for New York. Mrs MacRae, who happened to be a friend of Annie's, even helped the girl to pack for her voyage, little knowing that the man Annie was hoping to marry was her husband! But by then, MacRae had concluded that the only way out of the love tangle was to kill Annie. She was last seen alive on 20 July. MacRae murdered her and dismembered her body at the Dyechurch Lane warehouse, where her hair and bones were later found, before hiring a cart to drop the

legs off at Althorp. No trace of the baby was ever found –
except for the clothes.

Hardingstone Lane, nr Northampton

Scene of the famous Blazing Car Murder of 1930. On 5
November of that year, two young cousins were walking
home to Hardingstone after attending a bonfire party in
Northampton. As they turned off the London road into
Hardingstone Lane, they saw the figure of a man climb-
ing out of a ditch and further along the lane, a blazing
car. When the fire was extinguished, a badly charred
body was found across the front seat. The immediate
conclusion was that the corpse belonged to the driver
but the sighting of the mystery man and the position of
the body, which looked as if it had been thrown down
on to the seat, aroused police suspicions. The number-
plate of the Morris Minor was traced to 37-year-old
Alfred Arthur Rouse who lived in North London. It transpired that Rouse had killed a total stranger in order to
fake his own death. He had hit the man over the head
with a mallet and then pushed him into the car, which
he then set alight with a can of petrol. The reason for
such drastic measures was that Rouse, although married, had slept with nearly 80 women in his capacity as a
commercial traveller, a number of whom bore his children. Realising that his activities were beginning to take
their toll, personally and financially, he sought a new
identity. Found guilty of murder, Rouse was hanged at
Bedford.

Naseby: Hidden Well, Church Street

The Civil War battleground of Naseby was the scene of another bloody conflict in 1976 when former professional wrestler Diane Merritt was stabbed to death. Thirty-year-old Diane lived with her husband of 18 months and two women at Hidden Well, a large house near the parish church. It was alleged that Diane had made a number of attempts to kill her shopkeeper husband in order to claim his £50,000 life insurance and that when she heard that another woman had spoken of her plans, she lost her temper. In the early hours of 15 June 1976, there was a struggle in the house and Diane was fatally stabbed through the heart. She tumbled down the stairs and died. A woman was charged with murder but was eventually acquitted.

NOTTINGHAMSHIRE

Harlow Wood

On the east side of the A60, three miles south of Mansfield and half a mile north of Ravenshead, stands a small stone in memory of 17-year-old Elizabeth Sheppard who was brutally murdered at that spot on 7 July 1817. Wearing a new pair of shoes and carrying an umbrella, Elizabeth had left her home in Papplewick to travel to Mansfield in the hope of finding work as a servant. She was seen leaving Mansfield at around 6 pm but never made it home. Her body was found the next morning by the side of the road at Harlow Wood, her skull fractured. The murder weapon, a large hedge stake, was discovered nearby. She had been waylaid by 33-year-old Charles Rotherham from Sheffield who battered her to death for no apparent reason. He had been drinking at the Hut, a public house on the Mansfield road, on the evening of the murder and stayed overnight at the Three Crowns Inn, Redhill, in Nottinghamshire, where he had endeavoured to sell a pair of ladies' shoes and an umbrella. He was unsuccessful and left the shoes in his room and later sold the umbrella in the quaintly named South Notts village of Bunny. Charged with the murder, Rotherham confessed and was duly executed.

Mansfield: 1 Star Terrace, Commercial St

For an unknown reason, 35-year-old foundry labourer Henry Wright developed a strong dislike to the

Reynolds family with whom he lodged at Star Terrace in Mansfield. He expressed his feelings by massacring them in the early hours of Sunday 11 August 1859. His landlady, 48-year-old Mary Reynolds, was butchered, slashed and disembowelled. William Reynolds, 16, and Charles Reynolds, 15, were found with their heads nearly hacked off and little William Peck, aged 3½, was also murdered. The carnage over, Wright set fire to the house with the result that the small boy's body was nearly cremated. The *Mansfield Reporter* described it as 'roasted beyond recognition and so charred that when taken up, the body dropped to pieces.' Wright then survived an attempt to slit his own throat before wandering along to the local police station. According to contemporary sources, he stood there covered in gore and carrying a young child. He told the police to go to Star Terrace. Wright was executed on Christmas Eve 1895.

Nottingham: Colwick Woods

So popular was the hanging of 29-year-old murderer William Saville outside County Hall, Nottingham, on 7 August 1844 that 12 people were killed and over 100 injured in the crush to obtain a better view of his execution. Saville had incurred the wrath of the public by the most brutal killing of his wife Ann and their three children Harriet, Mary and Thomas. He neglected his family to the point that they were forced to go into a workhouse. In their absence and passing himself off as unmarried, he started an affair and asked his lover to marry him. The only blot on Saville's horizon was the release of his wife and children from the workhouse on 20 May 1844. They stayed with a friend that night but the following day Saville came to collect them, saying that he was to take them to relatives in Carlton. Instead he took them to Colwick Woods, on the east of the city, and murdered them. Ann was found behind an bush, where she had been dragged from a nearby spot where her children lay dead. In an attempt to implicate his poor wife, Saville had inserted a bloody razor in her left hand. Yet the hand itself was free from blood and witnesses saw Saville leaving the murder area without his family. In addition, there were bloody spots on his trousers and a quantity of mixed tea, belonging to his wife, was found about his person. The murder spot in Colwick Woods is still known as Saville's Spinney.

___

Nottingham: Sherwood Vale

The dream of 19-year-old clerk Leonard Mills was to commit the perfect murder. For his victim he selected a complete stranger, 48-year-old housewife Mabel Tattershaw, who had the misfortune to sit next to him at Nottingham's Roxy Cinema on 2 August 1951. Not that she realised it at the time for, flattered by his interest, she agreed to meet Mills the next day. On the evening of the 3rd, they went for a walk and sat down on grassland just off Sherwood Vale, to the north of the city. Having carefully arranged their coats in such a fashion that Mrs Tattershaw would be unable to pick up any fibres which could be used in forensic evidence, he put on a pair of gloves, knelt on her shoulders and calmly strangled her. Six days later, Mills telephoned the *News of the World* to report that he had just discovered a body, embellishing his story with mention of a sighting in the area of a sinister, limping man. Mills went on to tell that he had made his gruesome discovery while searching for a tranquil spot in which to compose a sonnet. But Mills' hopes of outwitting forensic science were misplaced. His hairs were found on the victim's dress and under her nails were fibres from his blue suit. Mills was found guilty of murder and sentenced to death.

Newark: Swan and Salmon Yard

In the summer of 1993, the peaceful market town of Newark, known for its medieval castle, acquired another, less desirable tourist attraction. For curious onlookers flocked to T & M Tools, a tumbledown workshop in the quiet Newark backwater of Swan and Salmon Yard, the former business premises of kidnapper and murderer Michael Sams. It was early in 1991, when with his business and third marriage in trouble, Sams, a railway enthusiast with an artificial leg, hatched his kidnap plan. He had already considered using an old railway line for the ransom drop and discovered the ideal location while exercising his dog along the Dove Valley Trail, a disused line converted for ramblers, at Oxspring, near Penistone, South Yorkshire. On 9 July 1991, he abducted 18-year-old Julie Dart from a street corner in the Leeds red light district of Chapeltown and sent a stencilled note to Leeds police headquarters demanding £140,000 for her release. On 19 July, Julie Dart's naked body was found in a field near the main King's Cross to Edinburgh line at Easton, Grantham. She had been hit on the head, probably with a hammer, and strangled. After making further threats to kidnap prostitutes, Sams struck again. On 22 January 1992, he kidnapped Birmingham estate agent Stephanie Slater. He took her to his Newark workshop and imprisoned her in a coffin-like box before demanding a £175,000 ransom. The drop was set for Oxspring. In the thick fog, Sams managed to escape with the cash and Stephanie

Slater was freed. But Sams had not been as clever as he thought. When the taped ransom demand to Stephanie's employers was played on *Crimewatch UK*, Sams' first wife Susan Oakes identified the voice and Sams was arrested the next day. He admitted kidnapping Stephanie Slater, but maintained throughout his trial that an unnamed friend had killed Julie Dart as she tried to escape. However, forensic evidence linked Julie Dart's body to Sams' Newark workshop and, in July 1993, he was given four life sentences for murder and kidnap. Mr Justice Judge said, 'undeterred by the horror of what you had done, you tried to turn her death to your advantage. The letters that you wrote make chilling reading; no qualms, no remorse, heartless at the grief you caused. Instead there was misplaced pride, callous arrogance.' After being sentenced, 52-year-old Sams finally confessed to the murder of Julie Dart at his Newark workshop on 10 July 1991.

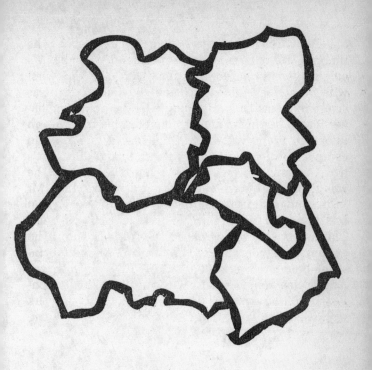

WEST
MIDLANDS

HEREFORD & WORCESTER

Burghill Court, Burghill

Elinor Drinkwater Woodhouse and her sister Martha lived on the 300-acre estate of Burghill Court at Burghill, two miles north of Hereford. On 6 September 1926, they informed their butler Charles Houghton that his services were no longer required as they thought he was beginning to drink too much. They gave him just 24 hours' notice and two months' wages. Evidently, Houghton was not impressed by their offer because the following morning, having served them breakfast, he shot the two sisters dead. He then went to his own room where he tried to cut his throat with a razor. There was no doubt in this case that the butler was indeed the perpetrator and his counsel somewhat lamely pleaded that he had a history of epileptic fits which effected Houghton's control of his actions. But the defence failed and Charles Houghton was hanged on 6 December 1926. Burghill Court still stands but is now divided into flats.

Cusop: Mayfield

Just on the English side of the Welsh border, less than a mile from the picturesque town of Hay-on-Wye, is the tiny village of Cusop, home to one of the century's most famous poisoners, Major Herbert Rowse Armstrong. A solicitor and clerk to the local magistrates, Armstrong practised in Hay and lived at Mayfield, a house in

Cusop. His vitriolic wife Katherine had been certified insane but after several months in an asylum, she went home only to then die in agony on 22 February 1921. The cause of death was certified as heart disease. That year Armstrong became involved in a dispute with fellow solicitor Oswald Martin over a land sale. One day, Armstrong invited Martin for tea and scones but on arriving home, he was taken violently ill. Martin's father-in-law, the town chemist, immediately suspected Armstrong, to whom he had sold a considerable quantity of arsenic, purportedly to kill the dandelions in his lawn. And when Martin's urine sample was tested, it was found to contain arsenic. The doctor prudently warned Martin not to accept any more invitations to tea from Armstrong. The case against Armstrong now gathered momentum and the body of his late wife was exhumed from Cusop churchyard to be found to contain arsenic too. It was revealed that a few months prior to Katherine's death, Armstrong had drawn up a new will for her in which she left him absolutely everything. Found guilty of murdering his wife, Major Armstrong was executed at Gloucester Prison on 31 May 1922.

Oddingley

Before the M5 was routed on its doorstep, the village of Oddingley, four miles north-east of Worcester, was a quiet spot in the heart of the English countryside. Such communities are traditionally close-knit and this was perfectly illustrated back in the early 19th century when the inhabitants closed ranks over the case of Richard Heming. It began in June 1806 when carpenter Heming killed Reverend Parker in a field at Oddingley. Heming shot the priest and made sure by beating him over the head with the gun. Heming then hid the murder weapon in a brown leather bag in a hedge. Heming was recognised by a witness but before he could be arrested, he disappeared from his home in Droitwich. The case took a significant turn when it was learned that Reverend Parker had become extremely unpopular with local farmers and the rumour was that they had clubbed together and paid Heming £50 to carry out the murder. However, in Heming's absence, this remained little more than idle speculation. Then, 24 years later in January 1830, a skeleton was found in an old barn near the Oddingley-Crowle road. It was that of the missing Heming. He too had been murdered, with a blunt instrument, allegedly by farmer James Taylor on the orders of Captain Evans, a major land-owner who was once a magistrate at Droitwich. But by 1830, Evans and Taylor were both dead so farmer Thomas Clewes and another man, George Banks, were tried for their part in the conspiracy. Both were acquitted. It seems that those who silenced Richard Heming had already gone to their own graves.

SHROPSHIRE

Hunkington: Moat Copse

Moat Copse was the location for the controversial murder case of celebrated rose-grower and ardent anti-nuclear campaigner Hilda Murrell. On 24 March 1984, the body of 78-year-old Miss Murrell was discovered on private land at Moat Copse, Hunkington, a little-known spot under the shadow of Haughmond Hill, six miles east of Shrewsbury. It was lying next to a tree where the nearest road, a lane leading from Haughmond Hill towards Withington, lay 500 yards away across a corn-field. Her car was abandoned nearby in a roadside ditch. Miss Murrell lived in a detached house at 52 Sutton Road, Shrewsbury, from where she was abducted three days earlier on 21 March. The evidence suggested that she had returned from a shopping trip at around 12.30 pm and disturbed an intruder. She was then driven in her car to Hunkington, dragged across the cornfield and stabbed repeatedly in Moat Copse before being left to die. The actual cause of death was hypothermia. The only item stolen from the house was the manuscript of a paper which Miss Murrell was due to present at a public inquiry into the construction of the nuclear power station Sizewell B. The question remains: Was Hilda Murrell silenced because she was considered a threat to the nuclear industry?

STAFFORDSHIRE

Barlaston: 'Estoril', Station Road

Wealthy pottery manufacturer Cuthbert Wiltshaw and his wife Alice lived in a splendid 14-roomed house christened 'Estoril' in the village of Barlaston, five miles south of Stoke-on-Trent. Mr Wiltshaw's chauffeur had been 29-year-old ex-Borstal boy Leslie Green but he was dismissed in May 1952 for using his employer's car without permission. Two months later, on 16 July, Green, desperate for money, broke into the Wiltshaws' house. Sixty-two-year-old Mrs Wiltshaw was preparing the evening meal when Green clubbed her to the ground from behind with two logs which he had picked up in the scullery. He then went upstairs, pocketed £3,000 worth of jewellery and came back down to rifle Mrs Wiltshaw's handbag. But by then she had recovered and staggering into the hall, recognised her assailant. At that moment Green's robbery turned into murder as he snatched a poker with a barbed end and stabbed her. He also battered her with a brass bowl and a china vase before grabbing Mr Wiltshaw's old RAF raincoat and escaping down the path to Barlaston railway station. It was the raincoat which helped to convict Green since when it was found, it had Green's blood on it. Additionally, footprints found on the tiled kitchen floor of the house matched Green's shoes. He was executed on 23 December 1952.

Cannock Chase

In the space of 19 months the bodies of three young girls were found in the Staffordshire beauty spot of Cannock Chase. The third, seven-year-old Christine Darby, had been kidnapped in broad daylight from Coronation Street, Walsall, on 19 August 1967 by a man in a grey car. Her nearly naked body was discovered buried in undergrowth on the chase three days later. All three victims lived within a 17-mile radius of each other, near the A34, and had been coaxed into cars while playing near their homes. Despite a huge manhunt, the killer remained at large for over a year. Then on 4 November 1968, a ten-year-old girl, playing on waste ground in Walsall, was approached by a man offering her fireworks. He tried to drag her into his car but she managed to escape. The vehicle was traced to 29-year-old works foreman Raymond Morris who lived with his second wife in Walsall, and who had previously owned a grey Austin A55. Morris was found guilty of murdering Christine Darby and was sentenced to life imprisonment. The two earlier murders remain unsolved.

Kidsgrove: Bathpool Park

Beautiful Bathpool Park in the centre of Kidsgrove, six miles north of Stoke-on-Trent, is a playground for the young and an oasis of calm for the elderly. But in 1975 it was the scene of one of the most chilling murders in the annals of British crime. Running underneath the park is a network of drainage tunnels and in a shaft leading down to them, police found the naked body of 17-year-old Lesley Whittle hanging from a wire noose. She was the victim of a killer known as the Black Panther. The

Panther was 38-year-old Donald Neilson, a family man from Bradford, who had already shot and killed three sub-postmasters during raids. After reading about her family's fortune, Neilson kidnapped Lesley from her home in Highley, Shropshire, at 4am on 14 January 1975 and kept her captive in the shaft at Bathpool Park. He demanded a £50,000 ransom. A schoolboy's discovery in the park of a strip of Dymo tape punched with the words, 'Drop suitcases into hole', led police to Lesley's body on 7 March. Neilson had pushed her from a ledge and she had literally died of fright. Neilson was arrested nine months later in Mansfield by two alert policemen and in the attic of his house were found a selection of knives, guns, ammunition and hoods. Convicted on four counts of murder, Neil was given four life sentences in addition to 61 years for kidnapping.

Rugeley: Talbot Arms, Market Street

The Staffordshire town of Rugeley's principal claim to fame is that it was the centre of operations for the murderous activities of Dr William Palmer, immortalised as 'The Rugeley Poisoner'. The outwardly respectable Palmer, 31, had a practice in the town but his main interest in life was betting on racehorses, a pastime which left him in financial ruin. He befriended racehorse owner John Cook, whose horse won the Shrewsbury Handicap on 13 November 1855, and afterwards by way of celebration the two men dined at the Raven Hotel, Shrewsbury, where Cook was taken ill after drinking brandy and water given to him by Palmer. The pair returned to Rugeley where Cook stayed at the Talbot Arms, opposite Palmer's house in Market Street. On 21 November, Cook died in agony following a visit from Palmer who had prescribed coffee and broth. While Palmer collected Cook's substantial winnings. Cook's autopsy revealed traces of antimony. Palmer was charged with murder and hanged at Stafford on 14 June 1856. He was also suspected of causing the deaths of 14 others, including his mother-in-law, wife and brother.

● The Talbot Arms subsequently changed its name to the Shrewsbury Arms but is now a wine bar called the Shrew. Palmer's house, greatly altered, is set back from Market Street. After his demise, it became the local Post Office but is currently a video shop.

Nr Wordsley: Yew Tree Farm, Lawnswood Road

The killing of 13-year-old paper boy Carl Bridgewater on 19 September 1978 has remained in the public eye ever since as those convicted of his murder have continually protested their innocence. Carl lived in Wordsley near Stourbridge and his round took him out of Wordsley and along Lawnswood Road, a turning off the A449 Wolverhampton-Kidderminster road. One of his last ports of call was Yew Tree Farm, reached by a track from Lawnswood Road. That afternoon, he was behind schedule for his final round owing to a dentist's appointment so he was slightly late arriving at the farm. There he interrupted a robbery and was shot dead by a single bullet from a shotgun. Four Birmingham criminals – James Robinson, Pat Molloy and cousins Vincent and Michael Hickey – were found guilty (Molloy only of manslaughter). Four weeks after their conviction, on 14 December 1979, there was another murder, at Holloway House Farm, the farm next door to Yew Tree.

WARWICKSHIRE

Alveston: Little Ham Bridge

On 4 November 1820, Nathaniel Quiney, Henry Adams, Samuel Sidney and Thomas Heytrey set out to rob a Mr Parker, the bailiff at Croft's Farm in Alveston where Heytrey worked as a blacksmith, because they knew he was going to Warwick that day to collect a considerable sum of money. So, with their faces blackened, they lay in wait for Parker at Little Ham Bridge, Alveston, a couple of miles north-east of Stratford-upon-Avon. But they attacked the wrong man, instead waylaying William Hiron who was returning from Warwick after voting in a by-election. The unfortunate Hiron was dragged from his horse, beaten and robbed. He staggered half a mile before collapsing and was found unconscious the next morning in a ditch by the side of Hunscott Lane. He died on 7 November. His assailants paid for their error with their lives.

Ashow: Dial House

The previous year, 21-year-old servant girl Ann Heytrey (brother of Thomas) was also hanged for murder. She killed her mistress, Mrs Sarah Dormer, by stabbing her in the throat on Sunday 29 August 1819. Heytrey had only worked at Dial House, Ashow (three miles north of Warwick) for four days when on the evening of the 29th, she was left alone with her employer. They had gone into the garden together to pick cucumbers and Mrs Dormer was sitting reading in the 'best kitchen' when Heytrey suddenly pushed her out of the chair, chased her upstairs to the bedroom and stabbed her with a carving knife. Heytrey tried to make it look like suicide but was unable to wash all the blood off her hands. She was found guilty of this apparently motiveless murder which was all the more mysterious for the fact that Mrs Dormer had earlier saved Heytrey from being condemned for a previous capital offence.

Bentley Heath

A 'queer-rolling' attack which went too far resulted in the murder of homosexaul hairdresser Thomas Walker at Bentley Heath near Atherstone. Fifty-seven-year-old Mr Walker, who lived at Polesworth, was found lying in a ditch beside a lonely lane on 6 June 1975. He had died from head injuries after being kicked and punched and he had also been robbed. His attackers had tried to hide the body by covering it with ferns. Mr Walker had met two men, one of whom had an artificial leg, in a Birmingham public house on the evening of 5 June. The trio drove out to Bentley where Mr Walker was killed around midnight. His car was later abandoned in St Helens, Lancashire. The man with the false leg was convicted of manslaughter but his accomplice was found guilty of murder and sentenced to life imprisonment.

Meon Hill

The area of Meon Hill, near the Tudor villages of Upper and Lower Quinton, has long been connected with witchcraft and the occult. At dusk on St Valentine's Day

1945, the body of 74-year-old hedgecutter Charles Walton was found under an oak tree on Meon Hill. He had been pinned to the ground with his own hay-fork, driven in with such force that it required the combined strength of two policemen to remove it. A rough sign of a cross had been slashed on the victim's throat. Police investigations were greeted by a wall of silence apart from dark mutterings about a poor crop despite good weather and rumours of Walton's mystic communication with birds. It was all too reminiscent of 1875 when at the nearby village of Long Compton, 80-year-old Ann Turner had been murdered and pinned to the ground with a hay-fork. Her killer, a youth by the name of John Hayward, had then inflicted a cross-shaped wound on her throat with a bill-hook. Ann Turner was said to have been a witch. However, a recent theory suggests that the murder of Charles Walton had more fundamental roots. It is alleged to have been carried out by a farmer owing Watson money who made the crime look like witchcraft to throw the police off the scent.

Stoneleigh Abbey

After his appointment as personal chauffeur to Lord Leigh, William Waite had moved with his wife Beryl and their two children to a flat on the Stoneleigh Abbey estate, south of Coventry. They were following in the family footsteps as Waite's father had once been batman to Lord Leigh. The Waites lived happily together for 14 years until the summer of 1966 when William Waite began an affair with a young typist in the estate office. At first, he contemplated divorce from Beryl but then concluded that murder was a better proposition. Early in 1968, he started to introduce small doses of Paris Green, an arsenic-based horticultural pesticide, into his wife's food and drink. She grew tired and thin, becoming a semi-invalid. Waite meanwhile maintained the image of a doting husband, carrying her from room to room whenever she felt sufficiently well to be moved. By 7 September 1969, Beryl Waite was desperately ill. The doctor left her a sleeping capsule which Waite administered to Beryl in the presence of her sister, unaware that he had previously emptied the contents and re-filled the capsule with arsenic. Beryl died in the early hours of the following morning, weighing just 6½ stone. Waite was found guilty of her murder and sentenced to life imprisonment.

Stratford-upon-Avon

A midwife at Tidmington on the border with Gloucestershire, 45-year-old spinster Olive Bennett led a double life. Although she appeared very prim, Olive used to catch the bus to Stratford-upon-Avon on her evenings off and visit local hostelries, chain-smoking and drinking large sherries. The night of 23 April 1954 was the 390th anniversary of Shakespeare's birthday and Stratford was full of revellers. Among them was Olive Bennett. She visited her usual haunts and was seen standing outside a hotel at 11.45 pm. It was the last time she was seen alive. The following morning, the gardener at Holy Trinity Church beside the River Avon spotted that a headstone was missing from the churchyard and nearby found a pair of spectacles, a woman's brown shoe and a set of lower dentures. Within hours, police had found Olive's body in the river, weighted down with the missing headstone. She had been strangled. Her killer was never captured.

Nr Warwick: Lawford Hall

Disgraced army officer John Donellan committed murder for the basest of motives – sheer greed. He wanted the fortune of his brother-in-law, 20-year-old Sir Theodosius Edward Boughton, and knowing that if some unfortunate accident were to befall Sir Theodosius, his money would pass to his own wife, Donellan set about poisoning his prey at the family home of Lawford Hall, near Warwick. Sir Theodosius was a poorly man anyway but his weak condition was not improved by Donellan's addition of deadly laurel-water to his medicine. No sooner had Sir Theodosius taken the medicine on 27 February 1781 than he made strange noises and started to writhe around and foam at the mouth before dying. Donellan washed out the bottles but his guilt was quickly established and he was executed at Warwick on 2 April 1781. Lawford Hall was demolished by 1795.

WEST MIDLANDS

Bilston: No. 4 Court, Coseley Row

Samuel Twigg was a difficult man to live with. Mary, his long-suffering wife of 15 years, had been forced to jump through the bedroom window of their tiny courtyard house in Bilston on a number of occasions to escape from his violent threats, but matters really came to a head on 25 July 1860. Drunk and swearing, Twigg, who was described by the local paper as a 'very bad looking man', lurched home around 1 am. Mary was in bed but was roused from her slumbers by her loving husband's proclamation that if she didn't cook him any supper, he would cut her throat from ear to ear. She duly obliged before returning to bed. Hearing another commotion, she went down to investigate and found that Twigg wanted a kiss. Mary tried to make her excuses and leave but Twigg insisted on his own way and stabbed her fatally with a pocket knife. Samuel Twigg was later hanged at Stafford.

Birmingham: Penn's Mill Lane, nr Erdington

Contemporary sources described 25-year-old bricklayer Abraham Thornton as 'repulsive'. Not the most glowing of references, but it did not deter him from gamefully pursuing the pure and virginal Mary Ashford at a dance. The dance was held at the Three Tuns (otherwise known as Tyburn House) in the Tyburn district of Birmingham on Whit Monday, 26 May, 1817. Mary went there with her friend Hannah Cox and soon caught Thornton's lusty eye. He must have made some impression because at the end of the evening, Mary and Thornton walked with Hannah and her fiancé along the Chester Road towards Erdington. Mary then seemed to part from Thornton and set off for her uncle's house at Langley Heath, taking a short cut across some fields. Her body was found in a water-filled pit in a field near Penn's Mill Lane. Her shoes and bonnet were lying at the edge of the pit. It appeared that she had walked through the field with Thornton, they had had sex and then she had drowned. Thornton was charged with her murder and the locals had no doubt that he had raped and killed her. He admitted being with Mary in the field but insisted that sex was with her consent. Thornton was found not guilty of Mary's murder but such was the loathing towards him that he was forced to emigrate to America.

Birmingham: YWCA Hostel, Edgbaston

A lunchtime drink led to a decapitation two days before Christmas 1959. Twenty-seven-year-old Irish labourer Patrick Byrne was working on a building site in Hagley Road, Birmingham, and that lunchtime he got drunk at the Ivy Bush public house. In the evening he hung around the YWCA Hostel in Edgbaston in the hope of catching a glimpse of one of the girls undressing. He could only see one light in the hostel, in room four of Queen's Wing, and peering through the window, he saw 29-year-old Stephanie Baird in her underskirt. When she spotted Byrne near her door, she challenged him. He tried to kiss her but when she screamed Byrne put his hands around her throat and pushed her back into the room, strangling her as he lay on her. He then cut off her head with a table knife. Police later found Stephanie's naked, headless body on the floor and the severed head on the bed. The motive for the murder was clearly sexual. Next to the body was a note which read: 'This was the thing I thought would never come.' In the meantime, Byrne had attacked another girl, in the laundry room at the YWCA, with a stone wrapped in a brassier which he had seized from the clothes line. She survived and Byrne returned to his lodgings nearby. Two months later, Byrne was arrested in Warrington. His handwriting matched that on the note and he was found guilty of murder and sentenced to life imprisonment. On appeal, the verdict was changed to one of manslaughter but the sentence remained unaltered.

Coventry: Broadgate

At 2.32 pm on Friday 25 August 1939, an IRA bomb exploded in Broadgate, a busy shopping street in the centre of Coventry, causing widespread destruction and the loss of five lives, including that of 21-year-old bride-to-be Laura Ansell. It had been placed in the carrier of a bicycle and ridden to Broadgate where it was left in front of a parked car. The bomb had been prepared in the front sitting-room of 25 Clara Street, Coventry, where 29-year-old James Richards lodged with an Irish family, the Hewitts, who were apparently oblivious to what was going on around them. In order to store his explosive, Richards even dug a hole under the stairs, to which the incredibly tolerant Hewitts didn't seem to object.

Richards and 32-year-old Peter Barnes were subsequently hanged.

Dudley: The Malt Shovel Inn

Crane driver Joseph Flavell was regarded as the village idiot of Dudley. He had a history of cruelty to animals and other members of his family suffered from mental illness. Twenty-four-year-old Flavell became bitterly jealous of his stepbrother James Bayliss who, at 14, was highly intelligent and seemed to have a bright future as an artist. The pair lived together at the Malt Shovel Inn, of which James's father was the licensee, until 6 March 1926 when Flavell hacked the sleeping Bayliss to death with an axe. He excused the deed by maintaining that Bayliss felt no pain because, 'I did it while he was asleep.' Despite doubts about his sanity, Flavell was found guilty of murder and originally sentenced to death, but this was later commuted to life imprisonment.

Walsall: Warwick Street

George Loake, a 64-year-old unemployed engine driver, had suffered severe migraines and extreme mood swings since suffering an accident at work during the summer of 1909. He developed an unhealthy interest in knives and began drinking heavily. His misery was compounded by the fact that he was separated from his wife Elizabeth who had gone to stay with the Dolloway family at Warwick Street in Walsall. On the morning of 7 August 1911, Loake made another attempt at reconciliation. They talked in the Dolloways' living room but the conversation soon degenerated into an argument. As

Elizabeth turned to leave, Loake grabbed her from behind and stabbed her with a knife which he had hidden in his coat. She died in a nearby courtyard. The murder was witnessed by 11-year-old Thomas Dolloway who raced upstairs and locked himself in his bedroom until it was safe to emerge. Loake was found guilty of murder and hanged at Stafford.

West Bromwich: Moor Street

In the early hours of Sunday 27 August 1933, Mrs Fox was in bed at her home in Moor Street when she was woken by the sound of breaking glass coming from downstairs. She woke her husband Charles who went down to investigate. There was the sound of a struggle before Mr Fox staggered back up the stairs and collapsed on the bedroom floor with a bowie knife in his back. The seven stab wounds proved fatal. The killer, Stanley Hobday, then coolly broke into a butcher's in nearby Bromford Lane where he used the butcher's razor for a shave and a needle and thread to mend a tear in the sleeve of his jacket, sustained during the murder of Mr Fox. He also had a drink from a milk bottle before stealing a car from a garage in Bromford Lane and driving to Cheshire. But Hobday had clumsily left his fingerprints on the milk bottle and was soon arrested in Cumbria after what is believed to be the first time in Britain that the description and details of a man wanted in connection with a murder inquiry had been broadcast on public radio. The appeal paid dividends for Hobday was found guilty and hanged.

NORTH-WEST ENGLAND

CHESHIRE

Warrington: Winwick Street

The testimony of a young man, whose conscience had plagued him for over a year, enabled the police to solve a difficult, open case. On the evening of 20 September 1954, 23-year-old machinist William Preston had enjoyed a few drinks in Warrington. Leaving the pub shortly after 10.30 pm, he passed on the road 63-year-old Arthur Bentley, who invited him into a garage on Winwick Street. According to Preston, Bentley proceeded to proposition him indecently. Preston reacted ferociously, stabbing, beating and strangling the old man before inserting a coat hanger into his throat and setting the body alight. The police were no nearer catching the killer when nearly a year later, Preston became involved in another fight. During subsequent questioning he completely broke down and confessed to the murder of Bentley. Preston was found guilty but insane and committed to Broadmoor.

CUMBRIA

Newton Arlosh

A remote rented cottage near Newton Arlosh, 13 miles west of Carlisle, overlooking the Solway Firth, was the hideout chosen by 'Monster Butler' Archibald Thompson Hall and his two associates following the robbery, abduction and murder of former MP Walter Scott-Elliot and his wife. Having killed the Scott-Elliots, Hall and Michael Kitto also murdered the third member of their gang, Mary Coggle, when she refused to part with Mrs Scott-Elliot's highly incriminating mink coat. The two men asphyxiated Coggle with a plastic bag and threw her body into a stream running under the Glasgow-Carlisle road. Having sold some of their ill-gotten gains, Hal and Kitto spent Christmas 1977 with the former's family but Hall's brother Donald, himself recently released from jail, took rather a close interest in the source of their wealth. So the pair invited him back to Newton Arlosh where they drugged and drowned him in the bath. The next day, they put the body in the car and drove to a hotel in the coastal town of North Berwick, east of Edinburgh. This was to be their undoing, for the hotel manager, not convinced that his guests would be able to pay the bill, phoned the police to check the car registration number. Finding that the number did not correspond with the make of car, they searched the vehicle and found Donald Hall's body in the boot. The game was up and Archibald Hall and Kitto were both sentenced to life imprisonment.

Plumpton: The Pack Horse Inn

Three desperate professional burglars, on the run after a robbery at a stately home, cold-bloodedly murdered one policeman and wounded three others in a 24-hour reign of violence which shook rural Cumbria. The burglary took place on the night of Wednesday 28 October 1885 at Netherby Hall, the historic seat of the Graham family, near the Scottish border two miles north of Longtown. The thieves escaped with jewellery but were challenged three hours later by police officers at Kingstown. Two policemen were shot and the men escaped towards Carlisle. A few hours later, a third policeman was viciously attacked with a jemmy. After lying low for a while, the men were spotted on the evening of the 29th near the Pack Horse Inn at Plumpton, four miles north of Penrith. PC Joseph Byrnes went to investigate and was fatally shot through the head in a field 200 yards from the inn. Two of the fugitives, Anthony Rudge and John Martin, were eventually overpowered at Tebay near Kendal while the third, James Baker, was arrested by an alert railway guard at Lancaster. All three were found guilty of murder and hanged at Carlisle.

GREATER MANCHESTER

Ashton-under-Lyne: Prince of Wales Hotel, Stamford Street

By one of those strange quirks of fate, James Henry Corbitt was a regular at the Help the Poor Struggler public house at Hollinwood which was run by the nation's most famous executioner, Albert Pierrepoint. And who should hang Corbitt on 28 November 1950 but *mein Host*? Corbitt, a 37-year-old toolmaker from Ashton, often used to visit the inn, situated on the Manchester-Oldham road, on Saturday nights in the company of married women. He and Pierrepoint were in the habit of greeting each other as 'Tish' and 'Tosh'. On the night of 20 August 1950, Corbitt left the inn with 33-year-old Mrs Eliza Wood from Oldham. The following morning her naked body was found in a room at the Prince of Wales Hotel in Ashton, five miles away. She had been strangled and the word 'Whore' had been scrawled across her forehead. Three months later, Pierrepoint was called to Strangeways Prison to execute his former customer. 'Hallo Tosh,' said Corbitt as Pierrepoint entered the cell. 'Hello Tish,' replied Pierrepoint. 'How are you?' Then he hanged him.

● After the murder, the Prince of Wales Hotel earned the nickname of 'The Strangler's Arms'. It closed as a public house in the 1960s and subsequently became an electrical shop.

Bolton: Turner Bridge

Evil Betty Eccles murdered at least three children simply to obtain the 50 shillings benefit from their burial funds. Harry Eccles had been left to raise two youngsters and a baby after his wife died in childbirth, and in January 1841 he married his second wife Betty. They lived in Turner Bridge, a suburb of Bolton, although Harry was away working six days a week at a mill in Manchester. In June 1842 a 10-month-old baby in Betty's care died, followed three months later by Alice, Betty's 10-year-old daughter from her first marriage. Both supposedly succumbed to fits. When two weeks later, on 26 September, Harry's eldest son William also died suddenly, the neighbours' tongues started to wag. A post-mortem on William revealed arsenic. The body of Alice was exhumed, with similar results. It was then ascertained that prior to marrying Harry, Betty had had two more children, Hannah and Nancy, both of whom died young. They too were exhumed. The body of Nancy contained arsenic but that of Hannah was too decomposed for accurate testing. Betty was charged with three murders. The court heard how William had been poisoned with damson pudding and a local shopkeeper testified that he had sold the defendant arsenic which she had claimed was to kill mice. Betty Eccles, one of the least known 19th century poisoners, was found guilty and hanged at Bolton on 6 May 1843.

Hyde: 16 Wardle Brook Avenue, Hattersley

Justifiably the most reviled murderers in the history of British crime, Ian Brady and Myra Hindley, were brought to justice following the slaying of 17-year-old apprentice Edward Evans at their home on the Hattersley housing estate on 6 October 1965. At 11.30 that night, Hindley called on her brother-in-law, David Smith, and asked him back to Wardle Brook Avenue. Smith had been invited there to watch the murder of Edward Evans, his head crushed by axe blows from Brady. Smith was horrified and phoned the police early next morning. They found the body of the dead youth in a bedroom. Smith added that Brady had boasted of burying bodies on the moors and a search of their home pieced together the details of their atrocities. A young neighbour of Hindley revealed that she had regularly gone up to bleak Saddleworth Moor, east of Oldham, with the couple. After an extensive operation, the bodies of 10-year-old Lesley Ann Downey and 12-year-old John Kilbride were found buried there. Brady and Hindley, the Moors Murderers, were sentenced to life imprisonment. In 1986, Hindley confessed that she and Brady had also killed 16-year-old Pauline Reade and 12-year-old Keith Bennett. The girl's body was found on Saddleworth Moor 24 years after she had vanished.

Manchester: Junction of Chorlton-cum-Hardy Road and Seymour Grove, Whalley Range

Small but immensely strong, Charles Frederick Peace was 19th century England's most notorious burglar. Years of successful break-ins turned to murder on the wet night of 1 August 1876 when Peace, by then 44, was spotted prowling around a large house on the corner of Seymour Grove, Whalley Range. He had been seen by policeman James Beanland who searched the grounds of the house, telling his colleague, 20-year-old probationary constable Nicholas Cock, to wait by the road. Beanland drew a blank but on his way out of the grounds, he heard two bangs and found Cock lying against the wall, shot near the heart. A young Irishman, William Habron, was found guilty of the murder and sentenced to death. Fortunately he was reprieved, for watching from the public gallery was the real killer, Charlie Peace. The day after the trial, Peace killed again and later confessed to the murder of the policeman, allowing the innocent Habron to be freed.

Manchester: Deansgate

Amid the rubble of a desolate bombsite in Deansgate, in the centre of Manchester, was found the body of 40-year-old prostitute Olive Balchin on Sunday 20 October 1946. Balchin, who had been staying at the women's hostel in Corporation Street, had been killed in the early hours, battered about the head with a leather-dresser's hammer. Her murderer was 39-year-old labourer Walter Rowland who was incriminated by his statement that he thought he had caught venereal disease from Balchin and so did not hesitate to strangle her. A habitual criminal, Rowland was lucky to be alive anyway. In 1934, he had been convicted of strangling his two-year-old daughter but the death sentence was reprieved. It looked as if Fortune was going to smile on him again when David John Ware, a prisoner at Walton Jail, Liverpool, suddenly confessed to the murder of Olive Balchin, but then he retracted his confession and Rowland was duly hanged.

Manchester: 1 Oakleigh Avenue, Burnage

Once a fine Victorian semi-detached house, 1 Oakleigh Avenue had been divided up into bed-sits by 1962 and was beginning to fall into disrepair (it has since been demolished). On the first floor lived 48-year-old William Nelson, a telegraphist at Manchester Victoria station, but on Easter Sunday, 22 April 1962, his mutilated body was found on his bed. The killer, having already sent anonymous letters to the police, then taunted them with a phone call. However he spoke too long and the call was traced to Manchester Piccadilly station where police arrested 22-year-old Frank Goodman who lived with his widowed mother at Radcliffe. Goodman pleaded guilty to the murder. He had met Mr Nelson in a public house, had gone to his home and battered him to death with a foot-long metal bed bolt before stealing his victim's £12 wage packet. Goodman also confessed to attacking Dennis Cronin on a train near Bury, robbing him of £10 and hurling him off the train. Cronin never recovered from his injuries and died three years later. Goodman was imprisoned for life.

Manchester: Car park of Manchester Royal Infirmary

Yorkshire Ripper Peter Sutcliffe strayed from his usual hunting grounds of Leeds and Bradford to claim his ninth victim, 41-year-old prostitute Vera Millward, in the well-lit car park of Manchester Royal Infirmary. A Spanish-born mother of seven, frail Vera Millward left her home in Moss Side on the evening of 16 May 1978, telling her boyfriend she was going out to buy cigarettes and to fetch something to ease her chronic chest pains. The next morning her battered and mutilated body was found lying on a pile of refuse in the corner of the car park. The gardener who made the hideous discovery thought at first that the body was a doll. Sutcliffe went on to kill four more times before his eventual apprehension.

Nr Stalybridge: Gorse Hall

The now-demolished Gorse Hall was an imposing, if isolated, mansion, standing in its own grounds overlooking Stalybridge. It was home to Mr and Mrs George Harry Storrs, who were distinctly wary of intruders following an incident with a gunman in September 1909. As a result, a huge alarm bell had been placed on the roof and two constables usually patrolled the grounds. But 1 November 1909 was the day of the municipal elections and this meant that the police were busy elsewhere. Consequently, it was easy for a young gunman to enter Gorse Hall unchallenged that night. There was a fearful struggle during which Mrs Storrs managed to wrestle the gun from her husband's assailant and race upstairs to ring the alarm bell but by the time help had arrived from Stalybridge, it was too late. George Harry Storrs lay on the kitchen floor, having been stabbed 15 times. He died shortly afterwards. Mr Storrs' criminal cousin Cornelius Howard was charged with murder and acquitted and later Mark Wilde, who in June 1910 had carried out a frenzied attack on a courting couple in a lovers' lane near Gorse Hall, was additionally charged with the murder of Mr Storrs. He too was acquitted and so the mystery remains. However, recent evidence would suggest that Wilde was lucky to walk free.

Werneth Low: Pole Bank Hall

The archetypal northern expression 'Trouble at t' mill' could have been invented for the Ashton family of Pole

Bank Hall near Woodley. Head of the household, Samuel Ashton, owned mills in the villages of Apethorn and Woodley, but there had been heavy hints of industrial unrest following the sacking of a young man called William Mosley from Apethorn in December 1830. Consequently, Samuel had handed the running of the mills over to his sons, Thomas and James. The latter was in control of Apethorn but on the night of 3 January 1831 he had arranged to take his girlfriend to Stockport and so 24-year-old Thomas agreed to look in to make sure everything was running smoothly. Since the family coach was being used that night by his father, it was on foot that Thomas left Pole Bank Hall at 7 pm. No sooner had he walked through the darkened grounds and reached the entrance to the Hall than he was fatally shot in the chest. Even the generous offer of a £1,500 reward failed to attract information, until three years later a convict in Derby Jail pointed the finger at William Mosley and his elder brother Joseph. William lost no time in turning King's Evidence, implicating 22-year-old James Garside who had paid the brothers 10 guineas each to help him murder any member of the Ashton family. Garside had done the shooting, the Mosleys' presence being to prevent Thomas Ashton from escaping back to the Hall. It was thus a contract killing for 30 guineas, Garside having been given his share and the gun by mysteriously anonymous men. Garside and Joseph Mosley paid for the crime with their lives.

Nr Worsley: The Jolly Carter Inn, Winton

On the night of 22 May 1826, two peddlers, brothers Alexander and Michael McKeand, were drinking in the Jolly Carter full of villainous intent. Landlord Joseph

Blears was asleep, leaving his wife to tidy up at closing time. The McKeands had decided to rob the inn and, at a given signal, Michael went to the bar and stabbed Mrs Blears in the head. Meanwhile Alexander marched upstairs to where the maid Elizabeth Bates and a young boy, William Higgins, were sleeping. The boy awoke to witness McKeand slitting Elizabeth Bates' throat. Higgins dashed out of the house and Alexander warned Michael, who left the knife sticking in Mrs Blears' head to go and search for the lad. The petrified Higgins hid in a dry ditch, just yards from the killers, but luckily they didn't spot him. Although Mrs Blears miraculously survived, Elizabeth Bates was dead. The McKeands lived rough for a week but were arrested after being spotted some 70 miles away, bathing their sore feet in the moorland village of Kitling near Kirkby Stephen. They were hanged at Lancaster.

LANCASHIRE

Accrington: 3 Warner Street

Fifteen-year-old Christopher Hindle was apprenticed to cabinet-maker and undertaker John Coates, who owned a combined house and shop in busy Warner Street, Accrington, as well as a workshop in Bridge Street. Just after 9 pm on the morning of 9 June 1896, Coates set off for the workshop, leaving his wife Sarah, aged 61, to conduct her daily chores. Coates then sent young Hindle on an errand back to Warner Street where, in a bedroom above the undertaker's, Hindle strangled Mrs Coates and slit her throat with a penknife. Hindle emerged from the shop and told passers-by that there had been a murder, explaining away the cuts on his right arm by saying they had been sustained in the struggle with the knifeman. But Hindle was a poor actor and was found guilty of murder, although his death sentence was commuted to life imprisonment. The motive for killing appeared to be to conceal the fact that Hindle was stealing from his employer. It is believed that Mrs Coates caught Hindle with stolen cash and was murdered for her trouble. The sum of £1 5s 6d was found hidden under a shelf with bloodstains nearby.

Blackburn: 3 Moss Street

Seven-year-old Emily Holland, who lived at 110 Moss Street, Blackburn, disappeared on 28 March 1876 after

attending school at Larkhill. Two days later her naked
mutilated body (minus, head, arms and legs) was found
in a field adjoining Bastwell Terrace. The missing legs
were later discovered in a parcel a mile away at Lower
Cunliffe. The torso had been wrapped in newspaper and
attached to it were wisps of human hair of different
colours and lengths. Naturally the police focused on
local barbers, among them William Fish, a married man
with two children, who owned a barber's shop at 3 Moss
Street. He was known locally as the singing barber. But
he didn't have much to sing about when police found a
burnt skull, bones and Emily's clothes hidden up a
chimney in the front room above his shop. Fish was
found guilty of murder and hanged. He had cut Emily's
throat with a razor and the story goes that he then used
the same razor on his customers!

Blackpool: 16 Regent's Road

The adventures of 'Brides in the Bath' murderer George
Joseph Smith continued in Blackpool. His second
victim was Alice Burnham, a 25-year-old nurse who had
first met Smith at Southsea in the summer of 1913. Once
he had ascertained that she was worth marrying, they
tied the knot in November, her life having been insured
for £500 the previous day. Smith chose Blackpool for
this murder but rejected the first lodgings because they
had no bath, an essential item of equipment for his
deadly designs. On 10 December, he settled on 16
Regent's Road, run by a Mrs Crossley. No sooner were
their bags unpacked than Smith had informed a doctor
that Alice was suffering from a bad headache. The
following evening, Mrs Crossley was horrified to see
water pouring down the wall in the kitchen. The cause

was soon apparent – Alice was dead in the bath, her head submerged. A verdict of accidental death was returned but Smith's landlady had her suspicions. As Smith departed her establishment to move on to fresh conquests, she yelled out down the street: 'Crippen!' Mrs Crossley was an astute judge of character.

Lancaster Castle

When James Bingham died in January 1911 after more than 30 years as caretaker and official guide to Lancaster Castle, his son Henry succeeded him in the post and invited his sister Margaret to be his housekeeper. Suddenly the previously health Margaret died and so Henry's other sister, Edith, moved into the castle. But Edith was so slovenly that Henry announced she would be replaced from 14 August. The Saturday before her dismissal was due to take effect, Henry was taken ill having eaten a steak prepared for him by Edith. He died three days later, the post-mortem revealing arsenic poisoning. Edith was charged with his murder and her case looked hopeless when she was additionally charged with killing James and Margaret Bingham after exhumations showed that their bodies also contained arsenic. The prosecution said that Edith had told her fiancé she owned the castle and feared that if she was sacked, she would lose him too. However Edith was nevertheless found not guilty.

Ribchester: The Joiner's Arms, Fleet Lane

Seventy-nine-year-old widow Ann Walne single-handedly ran the Joiner's Arms at Ribchester, a picturesque village seven miles east of Preston on the north bank of the River Ribble. The beer house was really nothing more than a cottage, the only bar being a table in Ann's living-room. On the night of 10 November 1862, a gang from Blackburn walked to Ribchester and robbed the Joiner's Arms. Ann Walne was struck over the head with a metal-tipped cane but the actual cause of death was suffocation after a woollen shawl had been rammed into her mouth to stop her screaming. Her body was found the following morning, her wrists tied to the bed-rail. The house had been ransacked. A stopped clock showed the time of death – 2.17 am. A reward of £100 was offered and a dubious local game-keeper known as 'Chorley Tom' named five men as being involved. Two of that number, George Woods and Duncan McPhail, were executed for Ann Walne's murder.

MERSEYSIDE

Knowsley Hall

Now a safari park, 2,500 acre Knowsley Hall, between Liverpool and St Helens, was the stately setting for two mindless murders in 1952. Harold Winstanley, a 19-year-old trainee footman, had worked for Lord and Lady Derby for ten months and had become a popular member of staff. On the evening of 19 October, while Lord Derby was away at a dinner engagement, Winstanley went upstairs to the smoking-room where Lady Derby was watching television. He was armed with a German stengun, acquired from a youth at Liverpool's James Street railway station. As Lady Derby turned to face him, Winstanley made her look away before shooting her. Although not mortally wounded, she lay on the floor pretending to be dead. Hearing the commotion, butler Walter Stallard entered and was promptly shot dead near the door of the First Library, to be followed by under-butler Douglas Stuart, gunned down despite begging for mercy. Half-way down the stairs, Winstanley encountered Lord Derby's valet, William Sullivan, who tried to escape into the garden. Winstanley pursued his quarry and wounded him. Realising he was out of ammunition, Winstanley went for a drink at the Coppull House Inn before handing himself over to the police. He was found guilty but insane and committed to Broadmoor.

Liverpool: Battlecrease House, Aigburth

This large mansion in a southern suburb of Liverpool was home to American-born Florence Maybrick and her English cotton-broker husband James who, at 59, was 23 years her senior. An incurable hypochondriac, James was healthy enough to keep a mistress, but when his wife also took a lover, James responded by excluding her from his will. So Florence decided to get her revenge and started poisoning him. She bought fly-papers and extracted the arsenic from them by soaking the papers in cold water. She claimed the arsenic was for a face-wash to cure her skin complaint. James's condition deteriorated until he died on 11 May 1889 and enough arsenic was found in the house to poison 50 people, let alone most of the flies in the northern hemisphere. Florence Maybrick was found guilty of murder but three days before her execution, she was given a reprieve and sentenced to life imprisonment. She served 15 years and died in Connecticut in 1941.

Liverpool: Bradfield's, Old Hall Street

The Liverpool Sack Murder, as it became known, took place at Bradfield's, a tarpaulin-maker's shop in Old Hall Street, on the night of 10 December 1913. Twenty-two-year-old George Ball worked in the shop with Samuel Elltoft, 18, and on the night in question, Ball battered spinister Christine Bradfield to death and stole the takings. He and Elltoft put the body in a sack, loaded it into a handcart and dumped the sack in the Leeds and Liverpool Canal where it was discovered the next day blocking the lock gates. The two youths had been seen pushing the handcart down the street and when Ball was arrested ten days later, he had bloodstains on his clothes and had the dead woman's watch. Ball insisted that Miss Bradfield had been killed by an unknown robber but he was found guilty and finally confessed while in the condemned cell. Elltoft received four years penal servitude for being an accessory after the fact.

Liverpool: Northbrook Street

Twenty-one-year-old playboy Joseph Reginald Clark had a hypnotic effect on girls. They were besotted with him to the extent that they were blind to his devious ways. At one time, he was the suitor of four sisters in Liverpool, each girl being blissfully unaware that he was involved with the other three. Then Clark met Alice Fontaine and went to lodge at her mother's house in Northbrook Street where he earned the pet name 'Teddy Bear'. He constantly borrowed money from mother and daughter until Alice stumbled across letters from another girl, claiming to be his fiancée. Clark was sent packing but the cuddly teddy turned grizzly and retaliated by sending Alice's mother obscene notes. One Sunday morning in October 1928, Clark suddenly appeared in Alice's bedroom as she was preparing herself for church. He tried to strangle her with a pyjama cord. She lost consciousness and when she came round, found that he had also attempted to slit her throat. Alice couldn't understand why her mother hadn't rushed to her aid. The answer lay downstairs. Mrs Fontaine had been strangled. 'Teddy Bear' was sure of a big surprise. He was executed.

Liverpool: 29 Wolverton Street, Anfield

A frightful murder committed in a dreary little terraced house in a quiet cul-de-sac led to the sensational trial of

52-year-old William Herbert Wallace, the man from the Pru. Wallace, a Prudential Assurance agent, had lived at 29 Wolverton Crescent with his wife Julia for 17 uneventful years. On the evening of 20 January 1931, Wallace left home at 6.45 pm, reminding Julia to bolt the back door as usual. He had been told to go and meet a man on business at 25 Menlove Gardens East in Mossley Hill. But after scouring the district, Wallace realised there was no such address. He arrived back home at 8.45 pm to find Julia's body in the sitting-room at the rear of the house. She was lying face down, killed by repeated blows to the head which had been so fierce that her brains were actually oozing on to the floor. Thinking that the journey to the fictitious address had been a cunning ruse, the police charged Wallace with murder. He was found guilty but the conviction was quashed on appeal and he walked free, only to die of a kidney disorder two years later. Officially the murder of Julia Wallace remains unsolved but recent evidence points strongly to young insurance agent Gordon Parry, a colleague of Wallace's.

Liverpool: Cameo Cinema, Wavertree

A real-life drama unfolded in Wavertree's Cameo Cinema on the evening of 19 March 1949 when two staff were shot dead during a robbery. It was around 9.30 pm when the box-office cashier heard six shots coming from the manager's office. On her way to investigate, she was almost knocked over by a masked gunman making his escape down the emergency staircase. In the office she found the manager, Leonard Thomas, and his assistant, John Catterall, dying from gunshot wounds. They had been counting the evening's takings. During the double murder, the cinema audience continued to watch the film, unaware of what was going on behind the scenes. An anonymous tip-off implicated Charles Connolly and George Kelly, two small-time Liverpool gangsters. Kelly was found guilty of murder and hanged while Connolly, who acted as lookout, was imprisoned for conspiracy to rob.

Southport: 20 The Promenade

A pillar of Southport society, 57-year-old Dr Robert Clements lived with his fourth wife Amy at a sea-front flat in an imposing three-storey block along the Promenade. Mrs Clements, an heiress who had been left £22,000 by her father, died on 27 May 1947. Cause of death was given as leukaemia but a post-mortem suggested morphine poisoning, and when it emerged that Dr Clements had prescribed morphine for a patient who had never received it, Mrs Clements' funeral was halted. A second post-mortem confirmed morphine poisoning. At this Dr Clements took his own life, as did the doctor who initially examined the body, horrified at having made the wrong diagnosis. A Coroner's Court ruled that Clements had murdered his wife. Suspicions were also voiced that he had done away with his first three wives, all of whom had money and whose death certificates were signed by their husband.

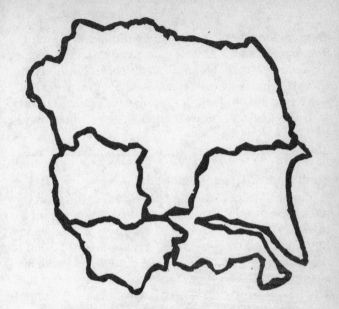

YORKSHIRE AND HUMBERSIDE

HUMBERSIDE

Hull: 4 Eton Terrace, Cambridge Street

Around the back of Paragon railway station is 4 Eton Terrace, one-time home of 50-year-old prostitute Alice Morgan. One of her regular customers was James Inglis, a 29-year-old Scotsman who lived at lodgings in Barmston Street in the eastern part of the city. He considered Alice a close friend but she saw him as just another client who paid her £5 for sex. On 1 February 1951, Inglis resigned from the Hessle shipyard where he had been working for just three days (one of a succession of jobs since his release from a mental hospital in 1945). He collected his wages and sought out Alice. That evening they drank in the Queen's Head on Walker Street and at the Victoria Vaults, just around the corner from Cambridge Street, before Inglis suggested they return to Alice's house. There was a major row, sparked by the fact that after drinking all day, Inglis could not afford Alice's services. Her body was found 36 hours later. She was naked from the waist down and had been strangled with a silk stocking during which five of her teeth had penetrated her tongue. It was a gruesome sight. She also had multiple fractures of the skull and a stab wound in the head, probably done with a hat-pin. Following the murder, Inglis viciously attacked a woman at his lodgings but she survived and he was arrested at Victoria Mansions, a Salvation Army hostel in Great Passage Street. Inglis confessed and, just before the judge passed sentence, said: 'All I ask now is that you get me hanged as soon as possible.' His wish was granted at Manchester on 8 May 1951.

Scunthorpe: 28 Kirkby Road, Riddings Estate

Married with a two-year-old daughter and a second child on the way, 23-year-old PC Graham Wood was also conducting an affair with a young policewoman. For the night of 28 June 1971, Wood had asked to be put on a different beat, claiming that he had investigations to complete. But the real reason was that he wanted to be near his semi-detached house in Kirkby Road. Between 1 and 2.15 am on the morning of the 29th, Police Headquarters lost radio contact with Wood. He had told his colleagues about receiving anonymous, threatening letters and when a fellow officer gave Wood a lift home that morning, Wood asked him in for coffee. Wood went into the bedroom and found his wife Glenis lying dead, strangled with the flex of an electric kettle. Partly hidden under her body was an anonymous letter. But Wood's plan fell apart and he broke down and confessed to killing his wife. He was sentenced to life imprisonment.

NORTH YORKSHIRE

Fewston: Primrose Cottage Plantation

The tiny village of Fewston is situated near the banks of Swinsby Reservoir, just south of the A59 Skipton-Harrogate Road as it crosses Blubberhouses Moor. For such a small community, it seems inconceivable that three major murders have been committed in the vicinity. In 1938, Fewston's village shop-keeper Margaret Peel was battered to death by an unknown killer; on 17 June 1982, Barry Prudom claimed his first victim by murdering PC David Haigh at nearby Warren Point; and on Coronation Day, 2 June 1953, 28-year-old Leeds car dealer Edward Watson was killed at Primrose Cottage Plantation. Watson's crime was that he had sold a defective car at a Harrogate auction, to which the purchaser, fellow dealer Robert Moore, had taken exception. Moore was determined to recover some of his outlay and lured Watson to the Harrogate area by telling him that a cheap car was coming up for auction that might interest him. To buy the fictitious vehicle, Watson came armed with £126. That was all Moore wanted and he promptly shot and robbed Watson and buried him in the woods. Moore then went home to Harrogate to watch the coronation on television. Police learned that Moore had recently bought a rifle and had been seen putting a spade in the boot of his car. Eventually he confessed and was executed at Leeds on 5 January 1954.

209

Grassington: Dibb Scar Glen, Grass Wood

Tom Lee was a brute of a man. He was not only the blacksmith in the scenic Wharfedale village of Grassington and landlord of the Blue Anchor Inn but he also liked to indulge in highway robbery. One attempted theft at Moor Lane, just outside Grassington, resulted in Lee being shot. His wounds were treated by Dr Petty who for some reason failed to turn Lee over to the authorities. However, Lee knew that one word from the doctor could send him to the gallows so, far from showing gratitude for the medic's discretion, he decided to silence him permanently. In such a far-flung rural community, Dr Petty had to visit his patients on horseback, his round of calls taking him over some inhospitable and sometimes sinister terrain. His route back to Grassington from Conistone was via Grass Wood and it was here, at Dibb Scar Glen, on the northern edge of the wood, that Lee lay in wait for him one night in October 1766. From behind a drystone wall, Lee leaped out and viciously attacked the doctor, secreting the body among rocks and covering it with vegetation. Knowing he would need to move the body, Lee bullied his apprentice into helping but when they returned to Grass Wood, they found Dr Petty still alive, crawling around. Lee finished the job with a series of blows from a large branch and the corpse was put in a sack and thrown into a nearby peat bog. When he heard that peat had the power to preserve human remains, Lee panicked and decided on another resting place for the doctor. This time coercing his wife, Lee tossed the weighted body into the River Wharfe at Loup Scar near Burnsall. However their clandestine activities were witnessed and the body was soon recovered. Lee's former apprentice told all, and the blacksmith was found guilty of murder and hanged on York's Knavesmire on 25 July 1768. Afterwards his body was left to hang in chains from a tree in Grass Wood.

Knaresborough: St Robert's Cave

Eugene Aram had an unusual combination of careers – Latin schoolmaster and petty thief. Aram lived in Vicarage Lane, Knaresborough, and his partner in these extra-curricular activities was flax-dresser Richard Houseman. On 7 February 1744, Aram murdered shoemaker Daniel Clark by hitting him over the head with a pick, to steal the £200 that he was carrying. He and Houseman then tucked the corpse beneath a rock in St Robert's Cave, near Grimbald Bridge on the River Nidd. For 14 years, their crime lay uncovered but then Houseman, hearing that a body had been found at Knaresborough, unburdened his guilt, in the process implicating Aram. In fact, the body wasn't that of Clark at all but by then Houseman had spilled the beans. Aram meanwhile was teaching Latin at the grammar school in King's Lynn but was arrested after being spotted by a visitor from Knaresborough to Norfolk. Eugene Aram had declined his last verb. He was hanged at York on 6 August 1759.

North Otterington: The Garths

Business consultant Timothy Franklin had become smitten with classy Tina Strauss while on a working trip to Jamaica. They fell in love and she came back to live with him in the village of North Otterington, two miles south of Northallerton. But the tranquillity of rural life was not for her and she kept threatening to return to

Jamaica. One day in 1971, exhausted by her temper tantrums, 43-year-old Franklin finally snapped. He smashed her face beyond recognition and tied a rope around her throat. He then buried the body six feet under the wind shelter in his garden. To cover up her disappearance, he informed friends that Strauss had left him for another man and once went to the trouble of flying to Jamaica to send telegrams in her name to her anxious mother and lawyer, saying that she was enjoying her holiday. However, when Franklin was quizzed, the dates on his passport were found to correspond with those when Strauss was supposedly holidaying in Jamaica. He was subsequently sentenced to life imprisonment.

Saxton Grange, nr Tadcaster

Isolated Saxton Grange farmhouse, near the village of Saxton, four miles south of Tadcaster, was the home of successful young businessman Frederick Morton and his wife Dorothy. Mrs Morton had been conducting a year-long affair with burly groom Ernest Brown who had blackmailed her into continuing the relationship. In June 1933, Brown packed his bags after refusing to mow the lawn but was soon reinstated – though only as odd-job man. Already insanely jealous, Brown was now consumed with venom at being given such a menial post and on the night of 5 September 1933, he exacted a full and bloody revenge. Having cut the phone lines, Brown paraded around brandishing a shotgun. The terrified Mrs Morton and nanny Ann Houseman barricaded themselves in the bathroom, waiting for the return of Mr Morton. Then at 3.30 in the morning, Mrs Morton saw flames leaping from the garage. The charred body of Frederick Morton was found inside. On the one square inch of flesh that wasn't burnt to a cinder were found shotgun pellets, inflicted before the fire. Brown had shot Mr Morton when he had arrived home at 9 pm and had later set fire to the garage. Brown was found guilty of murder and hanged in Leeds on 6 February 1934. There is a theory that Brown might also have murdered Evelyn Foster. On the scaffold when asked if he wished to make a confession, he supposedly said either 'ought to burn' or 'Otterburn'.

York: 30 Diamond Street

The naked body of 76-year-old Flora Gilligan was found on 10 March 1953 lying in the yard of her house at 30 Diamond Street, York. To all appearances, she could have fallen from her bedroom window but in truth she was the victim of a foul murder perpetrated by soldier Philip Henry of the King's Own Yorkshire Light Infantry. Henry had intended breaking into No. 32 next door but was unable to effect an entry and so climbed through the window of No. 30. Confronted by Miss Gilligan, he raped her and viciously beat her about the head, trying to make her death look like suicide, first by removing the shelves from the gas oven, and, when that failed, by taking her upstairs and pushing her out of the window. Although Henry had washed all his clothes after the killing, a distinctive footprint was found in the laundry basket inside the door of Miss Gilligan's house and a cobbler remembered repairing such shoes for Henry. The police swooped and Henry was eventually executed on 30 July. It was indeed fortunate that they arrested him so quickly since he was due to be posted overseas just nine days after the murder.

SOUTH YORKSHIRE

Dore, nr Sheffield

One of the most horrific massacres of the violent 1980s was carried out by 42-year-old petty thief Arthur Hutchinson who slaughtered three members of a wealthy Jewish family at their luxury home in Dore, just west of Sheffield. The day of 23 October 1983 started joyously for the family as they celebrated their eldest daughter's wedding, followed by a reception held in the marquee on the lawn of their home. Little did they know that their youngest daughter in particular was being scrutinised by Hutchinson, lurking in the shrubbery. Late that night she was woken by the noise of a struggle outside her bedroom door. Hutchinson appeared, saying that he had killed her parents. At knife-point, he forced the 18-year-old downstairs, past the body of her father, and out to the marquee where he raped her. He then took her back to her bedroom and raped her twice more. Both of her parents had been stabbed to death along with her brother. Hutchinson was eventually tracked down in a turnip field near Hartlepool and sentenced to three terms of life imprisonment.

Rotherham Technical College

A lecturer's obsession with a girl student led to a cold-blooded assassination in a corridor of learning. Scruffy Bernard Walden, a disabled 33-year-old physics lecturer at Rotherham Technical College, had proposed marriage to young Joyce Moran but she had laughed at the suggestion. After the evening lecture on 7 April 1959, the spurned Walden went to his locker, then followed Joyce and her boyfriend, 20-year-old Neil Saxton, towards the general office where he shot them both. Charged with murder, Walden told the court: 'I am not as other men. I am a cripple and must be armed to put me on fair terms with others ... I have an absolute right to kill.' Walden was duly executed at Leeds.

Sheffield: Banner Cross Terrace, Eccleshall Road

Fresh from his murder in Manchester, wizened little master-burglar Charles Peace returned to his native Sheffield to renew acquaintances with his old neighbours, the Dysons. Peace had lived near the Dysons in Britannia Road, Sheffield, and had a brief relationship with Mrs Catherine Dyson – no mean feat for a man who looked like a psychopathic gibbon. Her husband Arthur eventually banned Peace from the house to which Peace responded with characteristic vitriol, pulling a gun and threatening to blow the Dysons' brains out. In a bid to escape, the Dysons moved to Banner Cross Terrace but Peace followed them there. On the evening of 29 November 1876, Mrs Dyson put her son to bed and went to the outside toilet. Peace was waiting for her, armed. She screamed, her husband ran out and was shot dead by Peace in the ensuing struggle. Peace fled to London, living in 5 East Terrace, Evelina Road, Peckham, and passing himself off as a respectable family man. But his true identity was eventually uncovered and he was brought to trial and hanged at Leeds on 25 February 1879. Legend has it the crime rate almost halved overnight.

WEST YORKSHIRE

Bradford: Thornbury Crescent

When Elizabeth Barlow was found dead in her bath on the night of 3 May 1957, the initial evidence pointed to a simple case of drowning. Luckily the doctor noticed that the victim's eyes were widely dilated and two needle marks were eventually found in one of her buttocks. She had in fact been murdered by her husband Kenneth, a 38-year-old male nurse, who had injected her with insulin. Barlow had worked at Northfield Sanatorium, Driffield, and East Riding General Hospital where he had told colleagues and even patients of his fascination with insulin injection. He considered it to be the recipe for a perfect murder since it soon dissolves into the bloodstream where it is untraceable. Describing the joys of insulin, he had informed one patient at Driffield: 'Anybody gets a load of this, and it's the quickest way out.' Barlow was sentenced to life imprisonment for murdering his wife. He was released in 1984, still protesting his innocence.

Halifax: Congregational Church, Lister Lane

At lunchtime on 12 August 1953, six-year-old Mary Hackett left her home in Lister Lane, Halifax, to play nearby. She was never seen alive again, her body being discovered 40 days later in the Congregational Church just across the road from her home. Her killer was white-haired, 48-year-old church caretaker George Albert Hall

217

who had dealt the little girl repeated blows from behind with a blunt instrument and had buried her in the corner of the crypt. He had then piled chairs in front of the crypt and left two open paint tins to mask the stench of the rotting flesh. Hall was a talkative type but he made the mistake of talking too much. He had earlier been a patient at a mental hospital at Burley-in-Wharfedale and, in the course of conversation, he informed a doctor that the police had told him that Mary had died from severe injuries to the back of the head. But at that point, the police had yet to reveal the cause of death. Undone by his own tongue, Hall was hanged at Leeds in April 1954.

Huddersfield: Garrard's timber yard, Great Northern Street

The eighth victim of Yorkshire Ripper Peter Sutcliffe was found on 1 February 1978. She was 18-year-old prostitute Helen Rytka who lived with her twin sister Rita in a flat next to a motorway flyover. The Rytkas frequented the red-light district near Great Northern Street where the harsh railway arches of the Leeds-Manchester line formed a particularly dismal brothel. They preferred car trade and operated a system whereby they would wait for each other outside the public conveniences, one noting the registration number of the other's client. However the system broke down when, before Rita had returned from her customer, Helen accepted an offer from Sutcliffe in a red Ford Corsair. He took her to Garrard's timber yard. Unusually for him, he had sex with her, simply because he couldn't attack her until two passing taxi drivers had departed. As Helen Rytka made to get out of the back seat and go back to her sister, Sutcliffe clubbed her with a hammer and stabbed her before burying the body under a stack of wood.

Leeds: Back Lane, Horsforth

By their very nature, child-murders are utterly abhorrent but few have been more sickening than that of six-year-old Barbara Waterhouse, brutally butchered at Horsforth on the outskirts of Leeds in 1891. Her tiny body was found on 10 June in a cobbled yard at Alexander Street, Leeds wrapped in a tatty green shawl. Her throat had been cut from ear to ear, she had been stabbed a total of 46 times and she had been raped. Her killer was 32-year-old mill-hand Walter Turner who lived in Back Lane, Horsforth, not far from the Waterhouses. In an act that defies belief, Turner was assisted in the disposal of the body by his doting mother. She said she had found the corpse in the coal-hole of the house and had then bought chloride of lime to prevent any odour. She and her son took the body on a five-mile train journey to the centre of Leeds, transporting it in a tin trunk. After dumping the body in Alexander Street, Turner deposited the trunk on a platform at the Midland station. Mrs Turner was jailed for a year while Turner, who showed no emotion, was hanged. On sentencing him to death, the judge remarked that if the people of Horsforth had seen 'the way in which this poor little girl was mutilated, I am afraid that no power of the law, nor all the police in this town of Leeds, could ever have prevented them from tearing you limb from limb.'

Leeds: Amberley Road, Lower Wortley

Louie Calvert was a regular charmer. A thief and a prostitute, she persuaded house owner Arthur Calvert to marry her by telling him that she was pregnant. When Arthur became impatient that she was showing no signs of impending motherhood, she announced that she was going to stay with her sister in Dewsbury for the confinement. Instead she went to lodge with widow Lily Waterhouse at Amberley Road. Mrs Waterhouse complained to the police that Louie was stealing from her and was rewarded with a series of fatal blows on the evening of 31 March 1926. On the same day, a teenage unmarried mother, who had agreed to let Louie adopt her baby, handed the infant over and so Louie returned to her husband pretending she had given birth. Early the following morning, Louie went back to Amberley Road and stole some of Mrs Waterhouse's possessions. When police discovered the body, they arrested Louie who at the time was wearing the dead woman's boots even though they were several sizes too big for her. At the age of 33, Louie Calvert was found guilty of murder and executed. In the condemned cell she also confessed to killing elderly John Frobisher for whom she had worked as housekeeper and whose body had been recovered from a Leeds canal in 1922.

Leeds: Soldier's Field, Roundhay Park

The third of the Yorkshire Ripper's victims was 28-year-old Irene Richardson from Cowper Street in the red light district of Chapeltown. Richardson, who had taken to the streets after separating from her husband, left her home around 11.30 on the night of 5 February 1977 to go dancing. Within half an hour she was dead, murdered by Peter Sutcliffe. Her body was found near a sports pavilion in Roundhay Park, barely a mile from Chapeltown. It would be another four years and ten victims before Sutcliffe was finally brought to justice.

Nr Mirfield: Water Royd House

It was 12 May 1847 and James Wraith, an elderly retired farmer who lived at Water Royd House near Mirfield, a few miles from Huddersfield, was helping his wife prepare lunch. There was a knock on the door and servant Caroline Ellis admitted Irish hawker Patrick Reid. He asked her whether the household wanted any of his wares but before she could answer, he produced a heavy soldering iron from his bag and bludgeoned her to the floor. He then noticed Mr Wraith coming up from the cellar and hit him so hard that the soldering iron broke in two. Hearing the noise, Mrs Wraith rushed into the kitchen where she was ferociously felled with a poker. While Reid was searching the bodies for jewellery, another Irish hawker, Michael McCabe, knocked on the door. Reid managed to pass himself off as the householder and once McCabe had gone, ransacked the house and ensured the fate of his victims by slitting their throats with a razor. Reid then locked the house and threw the key and the iron down a well. However the massacre was discovered when a relative calling at the house that afternoon saw blood seeping under the back door. Reid and poor McCabe were charged with murder. Reid was acquitted for the murder of Mr Wraith but both were convicted of killing the two women. Finally Reid absolved McCabe whose death sentence was commuted to transportation for life – something of a raw deal since he was totally innocent. Meanwhile Reid was hanged at York on 8 January 1848 before an enthusiastic crowd of 40,000.

Scarcroft: Rose Cottage, Ling Lane

Now demolished, isolated Rose Cottage was a pretty, detached house near the village of Scarcroft, a few miles out of Leeds on the Wetherby road. It was the home of 65-year-old spinster Ann Barker who lived there alone. Around 10 am on 29 December 1948, a neighbour noticed that Ann's morning newspaper was still in the letterbox. Suspicious, she found Ann's battered body lying just inside the back door. Few people ventured along Ling Lane at night but a stranger had been seen there the previous evening. However this lead proved fruitless as did extensive interrogations of residents at a Polish workers' hostel in Wetherby. There was no obvious motive for the killing and the murder weapon was never found. In the circumstances, it is hardly surprising that the slaying of Ann Barker remains unsolved.

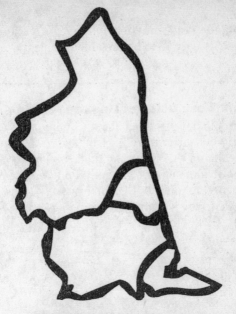

NORTH-EAST ENGLAND

CLEVELAND

Billingham Wharf
As the 2,000 ton SS Absalon moored at Billingham Reach on the River Tees, the thoughts of the ship's Third Engineer, 31-year-old Patrick Turnage, were solely on how best to enjoy his Saturday night on the town. Once on dry land, he sought the local knowledge of a bus conductor and asked him the best place to pick up a woman. He was told the Victoria Hotel in Joseph Street. There on that evening of 29 July 1950, Turnage met Julia Beesley who lived with her son in Nortbourne Road, Stockton. Julia liked to dress up at weekends and ply her trade as a prostitute – even at the age of 78! She ended up at the Victoria Hotel where the drunk Turnage, obviously mindful of any port in a storm, suggested they go back to his ships for yet more drinks. Turnage expected her to stay all night but it was a rule of Julia's never to do so. There was an argument that ended with Turnage strangling the poor woman. Her body was left in a ditch at the side of the lane leading from the wharf to the main road and remained hidden until the following afternoon. Turnage was very close to getting away with murder, for only a few hours later he would have been sailing away. Instead he was arrested. He pleaded guilty and was hanged.

DURHAM

Edmundbyers

Glasgow serial killer Peter Manuel only strayed south of the border for one murder – that of Newcastle taxi driver Sidney Dunn on the lonely moors at Edmundbyers, six miles west of Consett. Although Manuel had already secretly killed four times by October 1956, his prison sentence that year was one of 18 months for housebreaking at Hamilton. He was released from Barlinnie Prison on 30 November 1957 and eight days later he murdered Mr Dunn, who was found near his taxi, shot through the head and with his throat cut. It was only after Manuel's eventual execution following at least four further murders that a Coroner's inquest ruled that he had also killed Sidney Dunn.

Gainford

Elizabeth Pearson committed murder purely for the acquisition of a few sticks of furniture. Retired herdsman James Watson lived in a small house at Gainford, mid-way between Darlington and Barnard Castle. Following the death of his second wife in the spring of 1874, his finances necessitated taking in a lodger. So 28-year-old Elizabeth Pearson – his first wife's niece – moved in accompanied by her husband and baby girl. Their arrival heralded a decline in the old man's health, caused by Elizabeth sending her unwitting mother-in-law to buy a packet of Battle's Vermin Powder from a shop in the village. Elizabeth told her it was to kill an infestation of mice in the house but in truth it was to kill James Watson. On 15 March 1875 he died an agonising death and the autopsy revealed traces of strychnine, Prussian-blue ferrocyanic acid and starch – the precise constituents of Battle's Vermin Powder. Elizabeth wasted no time in laying her claim to the dead man's furniture but was stopped in her tracks when charged with his murder. She was hanged on 2 August 1875.

Holwick Fell

Cradled under rugged Cronkley Fell in the wilds of Teesdale, a couple of miles south from High Force, England's highest waterfall, is the isolated hamlet of Holwick. It is reached only by a minor road from Middleton-in-Teesdale and these days consists of little more than a few scattered farms and the Strathmore Arms. It was in a derelict hut near the inn and Hungry Hill Farm that elderly shepherd William Robinson lived back in 1794. He led a simple life alone with his dog – indeed it is said that he had never ventured beyond Barnard Castle some ten miles away. Yet one cold April day in 1794, William Robinson's body was found on Holwick Fell. His sheepdog was sitting beside him, frantically licking his master's face. But the old man was past saving – his throat had been cut. The motive for the murder was thought to be robbery since the deceased was rumoured to keep money in his hut, but the killer was never arrested.

West Auckland: 13 Front Street

Believed to be Britain's most prolific mass murderer, Mary Ann Cotton moved to a three-roomed stone cottage at Front Street, West Auckland, in 1871 with her bigamous husband, Frederick, his two stepsons and her own baby. Within a year, all were dead except Mary. It was the death of the younger stepson, seven-year-old Charles Edward on 12 July 1872, that aroused suspicions, although the post-mortem, held at the Rose and Crown Inn, next door to Cotton's house, stated natural causes. However a local doctor had taken the precaution of preserving the contents of the boy's stomach in a bottle and he found traces of arsenic. As a result, 40-year-old former nurse Mary Cotton was charged with murder. Investigations revealed that there had been an extraordinary number of deaths in her life. No fewer than 21 people close to her had died over a period of 20 years. She had given birth to 11 children of whom only one survived, a girl that she had given away. Exhumations of two of the other recent deaths in the Cotton household also revealed arsenic. Her defence claimed that Charles Edward had been accidentally poisoned by arsenic from some green floral wallpaper, but it became known that Cotton had purchased a mixture of arsenic and soft soap from a chemist in West Auckland in May 1872. The mixture contained 480 grains of arsenic – Cotton said it was to kill bed bugs. It was apparent that she had murdered the boy to cash in on his £8 Prudential life insurance policy and so that she could marry her latest lover. Mary Cotton was found guilty and hanged at Durham on 24 March 1873. The *Newcastle Journal* called her 'a monster in human shape' and local schoolchildren coined a rhyme that began: 'Mary Cotton, she's dead and rotten'. Nobody knows exactly how many she killed in her poisonous existence but the conservative estimate is around 25.

NORTHUMBERLAND

Nr Morpeth

Wages clerk John Nisbet left Newcastle on the 10.27 am slow train for Alnmouth on Friday 18th March 1910, carrying a bag containing £370, to be paid to the workers at a colliery near Widdrington Station, six miles north of Morpeth. When the train arrived at Alnmouth, a porter found Nisbet's body under the seat in a carriage. He had been shot five times. The cash bag had vanished and, emptied of its contents, was later found at the bottom of Isabella pit, a disused mine shaft near Morpeth. Nisbet's killer was 43-year-old John Dickman, a married man with two children, who lived in Lily Avenue, Jesmond. Not only was he familiar with Isabella pit but, a professional gambler, he was heavily in debt to moneylenders. Bloodstained trousers were found at his house and he was identified by witnesses as being Nisbet's travelling companion on the train. Nisbet had been seen alive at Heaton station, just outside Newcastle, and Dickman alighted at Morpeth so the murder was clearly committed somewhere between the two. Although neither the guns (the victim was shot with two different revolvers) nor the money was ever traced, Dickman was found guilty and hanged at Newcastle Prison on 10 August 1910. His name was also later linked to the killing of Caroline Luard in Kent.

Nr Otterburn: Wolf's Nick

The Northumberland moorland on the road to Jedburgh boats some of the least accessible terrain in England. It was across this barren landscape on the bitterly cold night of 6 January 1931 that 29-year-old Evelyn Foster was driving the family hire car. As she passed through Elishaw, a few miles north of Otterburn, she was hailed by a group of people sitting in a stationary car. One of the men asked to be taken to Otterburn from where he could complete his journey to Newcastle. However Miss Foster knew that the last bus from Otterburn to Newcastle had already departed and so she offered to drive him 25 miles further along the road to Ponteland where he would be able to make a connection to Newcastle. When they reached Belsay, six miles from Ponteland, the man ordered her to turn back. He became aggressive and seized the steering wheel. They drove back towards Otterburn until, at a particularly bleak spot known as Wolf's Nick, they stopped. There the man punched and kicked Miss Foster and indecently assaulted her. As she lost consciousness, he poured fluid over her and set fire to the car. She managed to open the car door and roll out on to the moorland but she died the next day from her burns. Before she expired, she described her attacker as a short man in a bowler hat. A Coroner's Inquest returned a verdict of murder but Evelyn Foster's killer was never caught. Indeed the police poured scorn on her story, stating that the man did not exist, the suggestion being that the victim accidentally killed herself while setting fire to the car for insurance purposes.

TYNE AND WEAR

Chopwell

Sturdy miner Abel Atherton settled in nicely at Mrs Patrick's lodging-house in Chopwell, ten miles south-west of Newcastle. But Mrs Elizabeth Patrick felt that Atherton, aged 30, was making himself a little too comfortable, particularly with her 15-year-old daughter. So she made him seek alternative accommodation. Undeterred, Atherton continued to call round, until one visit on 11 August 1909 erupted in to a major argument and he threatened Mrs Patrick. Seething with anger, he marched back to his new lodgings and fetched his gun. His new landlady tried to stop him but he threatened her too. When he arrived at Mrs Patrick's, she took one look at the weapon and, as if laying down the house rules, announced: 'You're not going to use that here.' A struggle ensued in the doorway and after one harmless discharge, a second shot saw Mrs Patrick fall dead to the floor. Atherton claimed the shooting was an accident but he was found guilty at Durham Assizes and hanged on 8 December 1909.

Felling-on-Tyne: Rectory Road, Windy Nook

Known as the Widow of Windy Nook, 66-year-old Mary Wilson was convicted of poisoning two men and is thought to have murdered two more. Mary lived in Windy Nook, a drab working-class district of Felling on the south bank of the Tyne. A heavy drinker, she killed purely for money. She had been married for 43 years to labourer John Knowles before she got the taste for poisoning. Although she was not charged with their murders, both Knowles and her subsequent lover, chimney sweep John Russell, died of phosphorus poisoning. Between them they left her just £46 – barely worth killing for. The crimes for which she stood trial were the murders of Oliver Leonard and Ernest Wilson. Mary found that Leonard, a 75-year-old retired estate agent who lived at nearby Hebburn, had money and so she persuaded him to come and lodge with her. They married at Jarrow in September 1957 but she wasted no time in poisoning his tea and within two weeks of the wedding, he was dead. He left her £50. Ernest Wilson, a 75-year-old retired engineer, was an even better prospect. He had £100 invested in the Co-op. Mary homed in on him and went to live at his bungalow in Rectory Road, Windy Nook. Two weeks after their wedding, he too was dead. Mary joked with the undertaker that she had given him so much trade, perhaps he could quote her a wholesale price! But it was no laughing matter when both bodies revealed traces of phosphorus. The Widow of Windy Nook was found guilty of murder but was not hanged because of her age. She died in prison in 1962.

Gateshead: River Tyne

On 10 March 1966 the body of 49-year-old, 16-stone Winifred Hepplewhite was found floating in the River Tyne at Gateshead between a Dutch vessel and the quay wall of the Baltic Flour Mill. She was wearing only a nightdress, cardigan, dressing-gown and elastic stock-ings. A leather belt was knotted around her neck and her ankles were bound together with plastic-covered cable. She had been murdered by her husband, 35-year-old Sheffield City Police Sergeant Kenneth Hepplewhite, on 31 January 1966. It seems that he strangled her at their Sheffield home, put the body in a sack, loaded it into his van, drove north and dumped the corpse in the Tyne. Winifred Hepplewhite was a nasty, vindictive woman who loathed her husband and had promised to wreck his career, while he was a dedicated policeman with an unblemished record. Hepplewhite was found guilty of murder but with a recommendation for mercy. He was therefore sentenced to life imprisonment.

Gosforth: Moor Crescent

An eminent surgeon at the Queen Elizabeth Hospital in Gateshead, Paul Vickers harboured political ambitions to which he considered his invalid wife Margaret to be a hindrance. Besides, Vickers had found a new love and acquired a mistress. So he decided to kill his wife, who was under treatment for schizophrenia, with an anti-cancer drug, CCNU. He made out false prescriptions for the drug in capsule form that he then had sent to him, changing the labels on the containers so that his wife would be unable to identify them. He administered the drug in her food at their home in Moor Crescent, Gos-forth, with the result that she developed a rare blood disease, aplastic anaemia, from which she died a linger-ing, painful death in June 1979. Six months later, Vickers' mistress turned against him and alleged that he had obtained drugs by criminal deception. The police looked into the matter and charged them both with murder. She was acquitted but he was found guilty and sentenced to life imprisonment.

Newcastle upon Tyne: Scotswood council estate

To some, the mere mention of the name Mary Bell still sends a shiver down the spine. For the day before her 11th birthday, she killed a four-year-old boy and two months later she struck again, her victim this time being just three. It was on 25 May 1968 that four-year-old Martin Brown was found dead in the upstairs room of a derelict house on Newcastle's Scotswood council estate. There were no obvious signs of any foul play but two days later, nearby Woodlands Crescent Day Nursery was broken into and childish graffiti referred to the boy's death. The same day, Mary Bell's contribution to the Delaval Road Junior School 'Newsbook' was a drawing that corresponded exactly to the position in which Martin Brown had been found. Mary also called at the dead boy's home and asked his mother if she could see him in his coffin. Parents on the estate knew Mary had a sadistic streak – the mother of three girls had previously complained to the police that she had squeezed their daughters' throats. Then just two months after Martin's death, three-year-old Brian Howe disappeared from the estate. A search revealed nothing until Mary told Brian's sister to look on a patch of wasteland known as the Tin Lizzie. His body was found that night. He had been strangled and superficial cuts – in the shapes of M and N – had been made on his stomach. The post-mortem revealed that the fingermarks on the boy's neck could only have been made by another child. Some 1,200 children were quizzed, among them Mary Bell and her close friend, although no relation, 13-year-old Norma Bell.

Each accused the other of killing Brian although they admitted writing the graffiti in the nursery. Norma was acquitted but Mary was found guilty of the manslaughter of Martin and Brian, on the grounds of diminished responsibility. Although she was sentenced to life detention, Mary Bell was released in 1980, just before her 23rd birthday.

Sunderland: River Wear

An act of murderous mutiny took place on the River Wear in the early hours of 12 June 1839 as ship's mate Jacob Ehlert battered his captain to death. The Phoenix, a Norwegian vessel, was docked at Sunderland when Ehlert crept into the cabin of the captain, John Berkhalt, and dealt him three fierce blows to the head with a hammer as he lay asleep. As part of an ingenious play of disposal, Ehlert slung a rope around the neck of the corpse and raised it through the skylight. Then, with the reluctant assistance of a cabin boy, who had been threatened with murder if he didn't comply, Ehlert lowered the body into a boat and rowed to the other side of the river. There, on this sinister, rainy night, Ehlert weighted the body down with a large stone and threw it into the depths of the Wear. But the captains's remains were found just two days later and Ehlert was subsequently executed.

Whitley Bay: Windsor Road, Monkseaton

It was a normal, quiet Bank Holiday Sunday, 30 April 1989, in the seaside suburb of Monkseaton and a father of two was delivering church leaflets along Windsor Road. From the opposite direction there came a young man dressed entirely in black and wearing dark glasses. He had a combat-knife strapped to one thigh and was brandishing a shotgun. As the man looked up, and without any warning, the youth fired both barrels into him. As his wounded victim begged for mercy, the gunman replied: 'No, it is your day to die.' And with that he shot him in the chest at point blank range. The innocent passer-by, caught up in one man's murderous fantasy, died and 14 others were wounded in a 20-minute spree of violence. When arrested, the gunman claimed he had been driven to kill by the voice of Michael Myers, the teenage psychopath in the film Halloween, and recalled making a pilgrimage to Hungerford, scene of Michael Ryan's massacre.

SCOTLAND

BORDERS

Maxwellheugh, nr Kelso

Margaret Dickson must surely go down in history as the only murderer to be married a month after she was hanged! The drama began when Margaret, separated from her husband, left her two children behind in Musselburgh, east of Edinburgh, and set out to visit two aunts living in Newcastle. By early 1723, she had reached the village of Maxwellheugh, just south of Kelso, and had accepted an offer of work from the Bell family. She decided to stay a while but the sojourn turned sour when, according to Margaret, one of her employer's drunken sons, William Bell, forced himself on her while she was asleep. The body of the resultant newborn child was found in the nearby River Tweed on 9 December 1723. Margaret claimed the child had been stillborn but since she had concealed her pregnancy, her case was not very plausible and she was charged with murder. Found guilty, she was hanged in Edinburgh on 2 September 1724. However, that was by no means the end of Margaret Dickson. For after the execution, a group of her friends took the coffin to her native Musselburgh. En route they stopped for refreshment at the village of Peppermill where a noise was heard coming from the coffin. Margaret was still alive. What's more, she recovered sufficiently to attend church on 6 September, the Sunday after she was hanged, and the following month it was reported that she had remarried her former husband!

DUMFRIES & GALLOWAY

Dumfries Jail

Born in 1800, David Haggart was a habitual criminal. He had been involved in pickpocketing or other acts of theft throughout Scotland and had spent most of his life on the run. Finally his luck ran out and he was imprisoned at Dumfries. There he joined in an escape plan hatched by others. The idea was to hit the turnkey over the head with a stone wrapped in a cloth, grab the keys and release all the prisoners. But during the escape, the jailer was killed by Haggart's blow. This time Haggart was wanted for murder. He managed to evade the authorities by fleeing to Carlisle, Newcastle, Dundee, Perth and eventually Ireland where he was arrested for pickpocketing. He was returned to Scotland where he was found guilty of the turnkey's murder. While awaiting execution, Haggart penned his autobiography and was then hanged in Edinburgh, aged around 25.

Nr Kirkcudbright

In the summer of 1780, a Kirkcudbright farmer and his wife returned from harvesting to find their daughter lying dead in their lonely farm cottage with her throat cut. The dead girl was pregnant and it was immediately deduced that this was the motive for murder since she had kept the father's identity a closely guarded secret. A shoe print found on marshy ground nearby matched that of a local labourer, Richardson, who also happened to be left-handed (the cut on the victim's throat was from right to left so medical expertise concluded that the killer was left-handed). To explain the scratches on his face and his muddy stockings, Richardson claimed he was gathering nuts at the time of the murder, but his workmates testified that he had stopped their cart near the girls's cottage that day. He asked them to wait while he went to the blacksmith's but when he returned half an hour later, his face was badly scratched. The case against Richardson was complete when it was proved that he was the dead girl's secret lover. He was duly executed.

GRAMPIAN

Aberdeen: 61 Urquhart Road

The bane of Jeannie Donald's life was eight-year-old Helen Priestly who lived in the flat above her. Helen relentlessly teased Mrs Donald, ringing her doorbell and running away, and from the time when a home perm went sadly awry, taunting her with cries of 'Coconut!' On 20 April 1934, Helen came home from school in her dinner-hour and went out to buy a loaf of bread for her mother. She was seen heading for home at 1.45 pm but then disappeared completely until the following morning when her body was found in a sack under the tenement stairs. She had been asphyxiated. Early diagnosis suggested rape but it is believed that this was an attempt by Helen's real killer, 38-year-old Jeannie Donald, to indicate a male murderer. The most damning evidence at Donald's trial came from her own daughter, a playmate of Helen's, who failed to recognise part of a loaf found in her home. It was a Co-op loaf, the type that Helen Priestly had been sent to buy. Whether Helen was killed as part of a lesson in discipline that got out of hand will never be known, but Jeannie Donald was found guilty of murder and sentenced to death although this was later commuted to penal servitude for life.

Lauriston Castle, nr St Cyrus

Max and Sheila Garvie lived with their three children at West Cairnbeg Farm between Auchenblae and Fettercairn. But their marriage began to fall apart as Max developed an unhealthy interest in pornography and in 1967 Sheila met 22-year-old Brian Tevendale. To make a cosy foursome, Max had an affair with Tevendale's married sister. On 14 May 1968 Max Garvie left home by car to attend a business meeting in Stonehaven and was never seen alive again. Bludgeoned and shot through the neck, his body was found on 17 August in an underground tunnel at Lauriston Castle near St Cyrus, a coastal village five miles north of Montrose. Sheila Garvie and Tevendale were charged with murder, together with one of Tevendale's friends, Alan Peters. The court heard how Tevendale shot Max Garvie while he lay asleep and a juror fainted when the dead man's yellowed skull was produced as part of prosecution evidence. The case against Peters was Not Proven but Sheila Garvie and Tevendale were found guilty of murder and sentenced to life imprisonment.

HIGHLAND

Culbokie: 'Dunrobin', Mounteagle Road

The Black Isle peninsula near Inverness is bordered on three sides by the waters of the Firths of Moray, Beauly and Cromarty. Most of the 'isle' is blanketed by forest, on the western edge of which is the village of Culbokie, population around 300. On the outskirts of Culbokie, separated from the dark, dense forest by just a small field, is a bungalow which in 1984 was called 'Dunrobin' and was the home of Elizabeth 'Totsie' Sutherland, her two children and her husband Kenny who in fact had built the bungalow. On Monday 24 September 1984, Elizabeth Sutherland's nine-year-old daughter arrived home from school to find her mother lying face down in a pool of blood in one of the bedrooms, having suffered multiple stab wounds to the chest and neck. She had been killed with a kitchen knife that had been washed and put back in its drawer although it still carried traces of the dead woman's blood. After a painstaking investigation, the murderer was caught returning to Culbokie to do another burglary on the edge of the forest. He was 30-year-old George MacPhee who lived at Crook in Durham but had been raised on the Black Isle at Tore. His accomplice told police that MacPhee had killed Elizabeth Sutherland when she came back unexpectedly to the bungalow and disturbed him. MacPhee was sentenced to life imprisonment.

Glen Affric

Petty criminal Archibald Thompson Hall made a passable butler and it was in this guise that he was taken on by former M.P. Walter Scott-Elliot in November 1977. Mr Scott-Elliot lived with his second wife Dorothy and their Knightsbridge apartment was bursting at the seams with antiques, a situation that was too good to resist for the thieving Hall. Enlisting the help of his former mistress Mary Coggle and another small-time criminal, Michael Kitto, Hall decided to rob the ageing couple on 8 December 1977. But the robbery went horribly wrong and Hall ended up smothering Mrs Scott-Elliot with a pillow. The evil trio then hired a car and drove north with the body in the boot. They took the confused Mr Scott-Elliot too and Coggle dressed in some of the dead woman's clothes so that when the old man was drugged, he would mistake Coggle for his wife. They dumped Mrs Scott-Elliot's body in a remote stream near Loch Earn, then Hall and Kitto drove back to Knightsbridge to ransack the apartment while Coggle looked after Mr Scott-Elliot at a rented cottage in Cumbria. Loaded with the spoils of murder, Hall and Kitto drove north once more, picked up Coggle and Mr Scott-Elliot and headed to the wilds of Inverness-shire. On 14 December 1977 they had reached a desolate spot in Glen Affric near the tiny settlement of Tomich, some 15 miles west of Loch Ness, when their captive asked to be allowed out of the car to urinate. As he did so, they followed him into the forbidding woods and partially strangled the frail figure before finishing him off with blows from a spade that they had bought earlier in Lanark. They then buried his body in a shallow grave, a miserable end for a gallant old soldier.

LOTHIAN

Edinburgh: Tanner's Closer

These days the West Port area of Edinburgh in the shadow of the castle carries few reminders of its grisly past – except for the Burke and Hare pub in High Riggs! For opposite this hostelry (ironically once a fun pub), on a site now occupied by an office, stood Tanner's Close, headquarters of the notorious 19th century grave robbers and mass murderers, William Burke and William Hare. A grim alley that got its name from the tannery at the closed end, Tanner's Close boasted a sleazy lodging-house at which Irish labourers Burke and Hare were permanent guests. Having found they could earn good money by body-snatching and selling the corpses, Burke and Hare decided to speed up the process by killing their own. Early in December 1827, Hare met an old woman named Abigail Simpson on South Bridge, about a mile from Tanner's Close. Her feet were aching, having carried her from Gilmerton, five miles south-east of Edinburgh. Hare lured her back to Tanner's Close, probably with the offer of whisky, and once there he poured more drinks in the small back room while Burke serenaded her with an Irish lullaby. The moment the poor woman dozed off, she was smothered. Transporting her body by the dead of night, Burke and Hare then sold it for £10 to anatomist Robert Knox at Surgeons Square, about 100 yards east of South Bridge. The pair committed at least 16 further murders over the next nine months before the law caught up with them. Hare turned King's Evidence but Burke was hanged in Edinburgh on 28 January 1829 before a vast appreciative audience.

Edinburgh: Stead's Place, Leith Walk

Paisley girl Jean Hamilton trusted Irish charmer William Bennison implicitly. In 1839 she married him, little dreaming that he was already wed to Mary Mullen whom he had installed in Airdrie. After Mary's death, Bennison and Jean moved into a dismal row of tenements in Stead's Place, Edinburgh, their spartan accommodation consisting of nothing more than two rooms and a closet. Thoughts that Bennison might now restrict himself to one woman at a time were dashed early in 1850 when he fell for pretty Margaret Robertson, a young girl whom he had met at prayer meetings. Embarking on a plan to murder Jean, he began talking openly about her ailing health and, to hasten her demise, he purchased arsenic from an apothecary in Kirkgate, Leith. He claimed it was to kill rats at Stead's Place. On 9 April he joined a Funeral Society who would pay towards the cost of any funeral and three days later he added arsenic to Jean's porridge. She died on 15 April 1850. Within a few hours of the death, Margaret Robertson was making tea in Bennison's kitchen, a fact that alerted Jean's sister. A post-mortem revealed arsenic and with no history of rodents at Stead's Place, Bennison was found guilty of murder and hanged.

Edinburgh: 31 Buckingham Terrace

Bertha Merrett had high hopes for her 17-year-old son Donald, a student at Edinburgh University, but little did she know that he had dropped out, preferring to study the female form. Each morning he would leave their house in Buckingham Terrace with his books dutifully tucked under his arm, only to spend most of the day at a dance hall in Picardy Place. On the morning of 17 March 1926, a shot rang out in the Merretts' sitting-room and Donald exclaimed: 'My mother has shot herself.' She recovered consciousness but was unable to remember precisely what had happened. She died on 1 April with the bullet still lodged in the base of her skull. The police discovered that to pay for his extravagant lifestyle, Donald had been drawing considerable sums of money from his mother's account. He was charged with her murder. The jury returned a verdict of Not Proven on the murder charge but found him guilty of forging his mother's cheques. He was jailed for a year. Perhaps justice was done in 1954 when, calling himself Ronald Chesney and on the run after murdering his wife and mother-in-law in Ealing, Merrett shot himself in a wood near Cologne.

STRATHCLYDE

Ardlamont House, Kyles of Bute

Overlooking Ardlamont Bay and the entrance to Loch Fyne along a dramatic stretch of Scottish coastline, imposing Ardlamont House is a classic setting for a murder mystery. Colonel Mustard et al would have felt very much at home here. But the question that still surrounds the events of 10 August 1893 is: Was it murder or not? It was then that 21-year-old Cecil Hambrough, whose father owned Ardlamont Estates, went rabbit-shooting on the estate with his tutor, Alfred Monson, and a man named Scott. There was an incident in the woods that left Cecil dead, apparently having accidentally shot himself. However, the previous day Cecil, a non-swimmer, had been the victim of another 'accident' when a boat containing himself and Monson capsized. It was learned that Monson had recently insured Cecil's life for £20,00 (he had unsuccessfully tried for £50,000) and when, with undue haste, he attempted to claim the money after Cecil's death, the police charged him with murder and attempted murder, the latter relating to the business with the boat. The prosecution claimed that Monson had shot Cecil Hambrough through the head as the youth walked along a dyke but the jury found the case Not Proven.

Biggar: St Mary's Cemetery

Fifteen-year-old Linda Peacock was a keen horsewoman and had spent the day of 6 August 1967 with her ponies at a farm near Biggar, a small town between Lanark and Peebles. A friend gave Linda a lift back to Biggar at around 8pm but at about 10.20 pm she was murdered in St Mary's Cemetery. She was beaten about the head, raped and strangled, the killing taking place in a particularly secluded part of the graveyard. Her body was found the next morning. Three witnesses reported hearing screams but the major clue was a bite mark on Linda's right breast. Investigations took in a nearby school for problem boys where one of the pupils was 17-year-old Gordon Hay. It was ascertained that on the night of the murder Hay had returned to his dormitory at around 10.30 pm in an agitated state. When the bite mark on Linda was found to match Hay's dental impressions, he was charged with murder. He was found guilty and ordered to be detained during Her Majesty's pleasure.

East Kilbride: 5 Fennbank Avenue, High Burnside

On the night of 16 September 1956, Peter Manuel and three others went on a burglary expedition to the affluent area of High Burnside, near East Kilbride, eight miles south of Glasgow. They broke into one house but when Manuel pointed out 5 Fennbank Avenue as a further likely target, his accomplices demurred. So Manuel went alone. It was the home of baker William Watt, who was away on a fishing holiday at Lochgilphead, and the only occupants were Mrs Marion Watt, her sister, Margaret Brown, and the Watts' 16-year-old daughter Vivienne. The following morning, a cleaning lady arrived to find all three shot through the head.

William Watt was arrested but released while Manuel remained at large for another 18 months, during which time he claimed at least five more victims. These included taxi driver Sidney Dunn, 17-year-old Isabelle Cooke in Mount Vernon, Glasgow, and three members of the Smart family at their home in Sheepburn Road, Uddingston. They too were shot through the head. When 31-year-old Manuel led the police to the spot where Isabelle Cooke was buried, he callously remarked: 'This is the place. In fact, I think I'm standing on her now.' And it became known that he had tested the gun that was to kill the Watts by shooting a cow through the nostril. Manuel was convicted on seven counts of human murder and hanged at Glasgow's Barlinnie Prison on 11 July 1958. Few tears were shed.

East Kilbride Golf Course

One murder which Peter Manuel admitted but was not convicted for (due to lack of evidence) was that of 17-year-old Annie Kneilands, found in a hollow on East Kilbride Golf Course on 4 January 1956. It is believed that Annie was waiting for her boyfriend in an East Kilbride street when Manuel came along in his Teddy Boy gear. She agreed to go to a nearby café with him but as he walked her home, he dragged her into a wood on the golf course and smashed her skull with a length of iron. Although her clothing was disarranged and her knickers were missing, she had not been raped.

Glasgow: 7 Blythswood Square

Architect's daughter Madeleine Smith had two ambitions in life: to elope and marry a Frenchman – one with a moustache. Emile L'Angelier, a Jersey clerk, who at 28 was ten years her senior, seemed to fit the bill perfectly but Madeleine quickly tired of his puritanical nature and became engaged to young Glasgow businessman Billy Minnoch. L'Angelier was appalled to learn of such a development and Madeleine decided to string him along for her own amusement. The Smiths had moved into a fine three-storey house, of which they only occupied the ground floor and basement, at 7 Blythswood Square. (The house has since been demolished and the Square is now comprised mainly of office blocks.) L'Angelier was invited to drop love letters at Madeleine's basement window while she passed warm cups of cocoa out to him. In February 1856, Madeleine openly bought arsenic, claiming that it to was to kill rats at the Smiths' summer home in Rhu. Shortly afterwards, her ardent suitor was taken ill, muttering about the taste of the cocoa. In one of her passionate letters, Madeleine begged him to visit her and so on 23 March L'Angelier set off for Blythswood Square in the hope of winning back his fair lady. Returning to his lodgings he was taken desperately sick and died the next day with enough arsenic inside him to kill 40 men. Madeleine Smith was charged with murder but the jury found the case Not Proven. She died in 1928 at the age of 93.

Glasgow: 131 Sauchiehall Street

Philandering physician Edward William Pritchard joined the ranks of notorious 19th century poisoners for murdering his wife and mother-in-law. Prichard was having an affair with 15-year-old servant girl Mary McLeod. He had made her pregnant and aborted her with a promise of marriage should his wife die. He set about keeping that promise by steadily poisoning his wife Mary Jane at their home in Sauchiehall Street. He tried various methods including aconite and lacing her tapioca with antimony. By the start of February 1865, Mrs Pritchard was so ill that her elderly mother, Jane Taylor, came to nurse her. Pritchard's welcoming gesture was to go out and buy another ounce of tincture of aconite. On 25 February Mrs Taylor died, Pritchard having added antimony and aconite to her bottle of Battley's Sedative Solution. Mary Pritchard followed suit on 18 March, prompting a theatrical display of contrived grief from Pritchard who insisted on publicly kissing his wife's corpse in the coffin. But an anonymous letter alerted the authorities to the possibility of foul play and Pritchard was charged with the two murders. Found guilty, he was hanged on Glasgow Green on 28 July 1865, an event for which the crowd began to gather the previous day, many sleeping on the Green overnight!

Glasgow: Prospecthill Road, Mount Florida

Murders by serving policemen are mercifully rare but one of the most famous occurred in the Mount Florida area of Glasgow in the early hours of 28 July 1950. Glasgow Southern Division Police Constable James Robertson, aged 33, was a married man who was also the father of the youngest child of 40-year-old Catherine McCluskey. On the night in question, Robertson slipped away from patrolling his beat for two hours and struck Miss McCluskey over the head with his truncheon before running her over in a stolen car. She was found lying in Prospecthill Road near the junction with Aikenhead Road, about a yard from the pavement. Robertson tried to make it look like a hit and run but inconsistencies in his story resulted in his being convicted of murder and executed at Barlinnie Prison on 16 December 1950.

Glasgow: nr Carmichael Place

The mysterious Bible John, so christened because of his tendency to quote from the Bible, remains Scotland's most elusive murderer. He struck three times in Glasgow in the late 1960s, picking up each victim at the famous Barrowland Ballroom. His activities first came to light when the strangled body of a married woman was found in a doorway near Carmichael Place on 22 February 1968. Then on 16 August 1969, the second victim, also married, was discovered in a derelict building in Mackeith Street. She too had been strangled. In a bid to trap the fiend, police mingled with dancers at the Barrowland but he struck again on 30 October 1969 when two girls headed home in a taxi from the ballroom with a man called John who had earlier slipped a Biblical reference into the conversation. One of the girls was dropped off near her home, the other was found the next morning, strangled behind a tenement block. Bible John has since vanished without trace.

Inchinnan, nr Paisley

Eighteen-year-old Christina Gilmour had forsaken John Anderson to marry John Gilmour on 27 November 1842. The newly-weds lived at Gilmour's farm at Inchinnan, a few miles north of Paisley, but it was hardly a conventional relationship. It was said that Christina hadn't consummated the marriage (nor even undressed) because her heart still lay with her former beau. On 29 December John Gilmour was struck down with stomach pains and vomiting. Then on 11 January 1843, just six weeks after the wedding, he died. The police learned that three days before Gilmour was first taken ill, Christina had instructed a servant to buy arsenic for killing rats and that early in January, using a false name, Christina herself had purchased arsenic from a Renfrew chemist. In April she sailed to New York but was extradited and brought back to Scotland in August. She was charged with murder but maintained that she had bought the arsenic to take her own life, not her husband's. The jury found the case Not Proven.

Isle of Arran: Goatfell

AT 2868 feet, Goatfell is the highest peak on the beautiful Isle of Arran and a rewarding challenge for climbers. On 12 July 1889, John Watson Laurie met Brixton clerk Edwin Rose on a steamer from Rothesay to Arran, twenty-five-year-old Laurie introducing himself as 'John Annandale'. The two struck up a friendship and three days later set out to conquer Goatfell. But Rose never came down, his body being found on 4 August buried under boulders in a spot known as Coire-na-fuhren (Gulley of fire). It seemed that his killer had pushed him from a precipice, clambered down and finished him off with a blow from a rock. Rose had also been robbed. After a huge manhunt, the mysterious 'Annandale' was eventually arrested back on the mainland in a wood near Ferniegair station. Laurie admitted robbing Rose but claimed that he had fallen accidentally. But Laurie was found guilty of murder and sentenced to death, only to be reprieved on grounds of insanity. He died in Perth Prison in 1930. His sole comment on the murder was: 'Rose hadn't very much, after all.'

TAYSIDE

Broughty Ferry: Elmgrove House, Grove Road

This 14-room mansion standing in two acres of grounds
and shielded from the outside world by a line of tall trees
and shrubs provided the truly sinister setting for the
Broughty Ferry Mystery of 1912. The sole occupant of
the house was eccentric 65-year-old spinster Jean Milne,
sister and heiress of a wealthy Dundee tobacco magnate.
On Saturday 2 November 1912 the postman at Broughty
Ferry (a coastal area on the Tay estuary, just east of Dundee) noticed that the letter-box at Elmgrove House was
overflowing with mail. He told the police who found the
body of Miss Milne lying at the foot of the stairs. She had
been beaten around the head with a poker and her
ankles had been bound together with a curtain-cord.
Garden shears had been used to cut the telephone wires.
Miss Milne was last seen alive on 15 October and therefore could well have lain dead for some three weeks. Yet
a strange woman was seen at a window of the house on
21 October. Rumours abounded that Miss Milne had a
mystery sweetheart and of a man being seen in the vicinity; but, despite intensive inquiries, the murder of Jean
Milne remains unsolved to this day.

Kenmore: Tower Cottage

Six miles west of Aberfeldy at the head of Loch Tay is
the little village of Kenmore. And in isolated Tower Cottage on the lower slopes of Kenmore Hill once lived the

McIntyre family. But on 26 September 1947, Mrs Catherine McIntyre's son came home for lunch to find her lying dead on her bed. She had been battered about the head and various articles had been stolen. In an area of bracken near the house, the police found the killer's hideout. There was a sawn-off shotgun with blood on the butt, a blood-stained handkerchief, a discarded razor-blade and, most important of all, a railway ticket of the type issued only to uniformed soldiers. The ticket led to Polish army deserter Stanislaw Myskza who, when arrested after a hectic chase, had Mrs McIntyre's wedding ring hidden in his shoe. It became known that he had stolen the shotgun whilst working on a nearby farm. Myszka was found guilty of murder at Perth.

WESTERN ISLES

Isle of Lewis

Murder is very much a rarity among the scattered crofters and fishermen of the sparsely populated Outer Hebrides but a capital crime did take place on the Isle of Lewis during the 19th century. Fisherman Malcolm McLean was convinced that his wife was going to kill him, so naturally he decided to get in first! All day he tried to pluck up courage until, sitting opposite her in their house, he suddenly grabbed her by the throat and strangled her. Shocked by what he had done, he wandered around aimlessly before going to Stornoway to give himself up. He confessed to the murder but his defence counsel pleaded that McLean was clearly insane. Unfortunately, this cut no ice with judge or jury and he was executed on 11 May 1838.

WALES

CLWYD

Penyffordd: Model Farm

William Brennan, a 27-year-old Irishman, was a new-comer in the North Wales community of Penyffordd, seven miles north of Wrexham. He had recently moved in to the village to live with his parents and decided to liven up the day of 5 March 1925 by shooting rabbits on Model Farm. However he was caught in the act by farmer John Rowlands, who tried to confiscate his shot-gun. Brennan offered to pay for the rabbits but flatly refused to surrender the gun. There was a struggle during which the gun went off. No one was hurt but in a blinding rage, Brennan reloaded and shot the farmer dead. Making his escape across the fields, he threatened a chasing labourer before hiding the weapon down a drain. Brennan was found guilty though insane and committed to Broadmoor.

Rhyl: 35 Kinmel Street

For years Sarah Jane Harvey had taken in lodgers at her small, two-storeyed terraced house at 35 Kinmel Street, Rhyl. In April 1960, Mrs Harvey was taken ill and had to go to hospital. Her son Leslie came over from his home in nearby Abergele and took the opportunity to redec-orate. But in the process he discovered a woman's body doubled up in a cupboard on a first-floor landing. The clothing was encrusted in cobwebs but was still recognisable as a nightdress and dressing-gown. The remains of what appeared to be a lisle stocking around the dead woman's neck led pathologists to the conclusion that she had been strangled. The woman turned out to be Mrs Frances Alice Knight, a frail old lady who had paid Mrs Harvey 30s a week to stay there in the 1930s. Leslie Harvey recalled his mother once saying that Mrs Knight had left in 1940. It also came to light that Mrs Harvey had been collecting the deceased's £2 maintenance money each week for the past 20 years, explaining that her lodger was housebound. This amounted to a grand total of over £2,000. As a result, 65-year-old Mrs Harvey was charged with murder. She insisted that Mrs Knight had died of natural causes and after five days the judge had to stop the trial, saying that the prosecution could not unquestionably prove that it had been murder. As a result Mrs Harvey was found guilty only of fraudulently obtaining money.

DYFED

Cwmdu: Cafn Hendre Farm

Somewhere in the hills and valleys around Llandeilo lies the remains of murdered Pole Stanislaw Sykut, killed 40 years ago by his business partner and country-man Michal Onufrejczyk. For although 59-year-old Onufrejczyk was sentenced to life imprisonment for murder, Sykut's body has never been found. The two Poles ran ramshackle Cafn Hendre Farm, half a mile from the village of Cwmdu and just over five miles north of the nearest town, Llandeilo. There was a considerable tension between the pair and eventually the hard-work-ing Sykut instructed a solicitor to draw up papers to terminate the partnership. Sykut had invested £600 and the solicitor's letter informed Onufrejczyk that unless Sykut's share was paid back in full, the farm would be put up to auction. Onufrejczyk was furious for there was no way he could raise that amount of money. Then be-tween 14 and 16 December 1953, Stanislaw Sykut disappeared off the face of the earth. Rumours reached the ears of the Sheriff's Officer but Onufrejczyk flatly re-fused to allow him to search the farm. Eventually the police came armed with a warrant and found tiny blood-stains in the kitchen and on the walls of the passage leading to the farmyard. Two minute fragments of bone were discovered near the fireplace in the kitchen. It was sufficient for Onufrejczyk to be convicted. But what became of Sykut? Rumour has it that his body was dismembered and buried in the bog which covered most of the farm – and local superstition says the bog is bottomless.

Nr Haverfordwest: Cuckoo Lane

A bizarre explosion in which a husband killed his wife and son and, inadvertently, himself shook the peaceful west Wales community of Haverfordwest back in September 1913. John Vaughan, a 46-year-old mole catcher, lived with his wife and son John, aged eight, in a cottage in Cuckoo Lane, just off the main road to Broad Haven, about a mile outside Haverfordwest. Vaughan suspected his wife of having an affair and decided to kill her and their son. So, while Mrs Vaughan was attending a Sunday evening service in Haverfordwest, Vaughan placed a dynamite cartridge and a fuse beneath the family bed. Just after 3 am on that fine moonlit night, Vaughan climbed out of bed in what was described as 'a premeditated, if mad, fit of jealousy', lit the fuse to the dynamite under his sleeping wife and child and made a run for the cottage door. But he barely reached it before the dynamite exploded. He was found bleeding profusely, his jaw almost severed, some ten yards from the front door. He died shortly afterwards. The dead bodies of Mrs Vaughan and young John were pulled out from a pile of rubble in the bedroom. Most of the cottage and three lives had been totally destroyed.

Nr Llangynin: Cadno Farm

On the evening of Friday 16 October 1953, John and Phoebe Harries of Derlwyn Farm, Llangynin, three miles north of St Clears, attended a Harvest Thanksgiving Service at the local Bryn Chapel. That was the last anybody saw of them. Their 24-year-old nephew Ronald said that he had driven them to Carmarthen railway station for a secret holiday in London and that they had left the farm in his capable hands. But the police were not convinced about the holiday story. For a start there was an uncooked joint of meat in Phoebe Harries's oven, an unlikely state of affairs for someone about to go off on holiday. Ronald Harries (John was his adopted uncle) lived at nearby Cadno Farm and it was there, buried in a kale field, that the bodies were finally found on 16 November. Convinced that Ronald was their man, detectives had tied cotton threads across the gaps in the hedges around Cadno. He panicked himself into thinking they had uncovered his secret and inspected the graves in the dead of night. At dawn, the police found where the thread was broken and it led them to John and Phoebe Harries. Ronald had borrowed a hammer from a neighbour on the night of the murders and had bludgeoned his aunt and uncle to death with it so that he could take over their farm. He had never returned the hammer – it was found hidden in undergrowth near Cadno Farm. Ronald Harries, who had killed solely for greed, was found guilty of murder and hanged at Swansea Prison.

Steynton: Scoveston Park

Reached by a bumpy lane, isolated Scoveston Park was a large run-down old country house near Steynton, a tiny village two miles north of Milford Haven. For all their lives, it had been the home of Richard Thomas and his sister Helen, both of whom were unmarried and in their

50s. Then on the night of Sunday 22 December 1985, a huge fire engulfed the house. Inside were found the bodies of Richard, on the first-floor landing, and Helen buried beneath a pile of rubble in the study. It appeared that she had been in the bedroom when the fire had started and had crashed with it into the study below. But this was no ordinary fire. For Richard and Helen had both been shot in the head and Helen had also been gagged, bound and blindfolded. Despite widespread appeals, the case remains unsolved.

GWENT

Llangybi

It was like a scene from *The Texas Chainsaw Massacre* except that it happened in a quiet corner of Gwent. All five members of the Watkins family had been savagely slain in a senseless blood-letting at their remote cottage outside Llangybi, six miles north of Newport. The head of the house, farm labourer William Watkins, was found lying on the garden path face down in a bed of Sweet William. He had been struck on the head with a heavy fencing post and stabbed repeatedly. There was a five-inch wound in his throat. Nearby lay his wife Elizabeth, brutally stabbed in the chest and her throat cut. Upstairs in the ransacked cottage, four-year-old Alice Watkins had been butchered in her bedroom. In another bedroom, six-year-old Frederick lay dead with his throat cut and eight-year-old Charlotte was slumped by an open window, having been frenziedly stabbed in the back presumably while trying to scream for help. The murderer had then attempted to conceal his wickedness by burning down the cottage. The man responsible for this outrage was 21-year-old Spanish seaman Joseph Garcia who had been released from Usk Prison, having completed a nine-month sentence for housebreaking, on 15 July 1878. By mid-afternoon he had reached Llangybi and, in a state of exhaustion, fell asleep next to a stile for around four hours. Sometime that night, he went to the Watkins' cottage, probably to beg for food. There, for no apparent reason, he massacred the family. Arrested at Newport railway station, Garcia was executed in November 1878.

Pontllanfraith: Fleur-de-Lys Avenue

Seventy-year-old spinster Blanche Matthews lived alone with her six cats in a house in Fleur-de-Lys Avenue, Pontllanfraith, situated in the Welsh valleys between Blackwood and Newbridge. She was so terrified of burglars that she had taken steps to turn her house into a fortress. However on 19 November 1955, she was attacked by a man who had broken in through a window. She was found on her bed, suffering from nine broken ribs, cuts, bruises and a throat wound – she died in hospital two days later. A local policeman remembered that on the evening of the murder he had encountered 21-year-old labourer William Edmunds who had explained his blood-splattered clothing by saying he had been in a fight. When Edmunds' flat was searched, police found two rings stolen from the dead woman. Edmunds was found guilty of murder and sentenced to life imprisonment.

GWYNEDD

Nr Dolgellau: Parc Farm

In July 1877, a little girl on an errand for her mother spotted a human arm in the River Arran as she crossed the wooden bridge between Pant-yr-Arran and Felin Ucha. At a bridge further up the river in the own of Dolgellau, searchers found lungs, entrails and a liver. The body was that of 36-year-old Sarah Hughes, an unmarried mother of two children. She had been bludgeoned to death in a fit of passion by her married lover, 26-year-old Cadwaladr Jones, on 4 June 1877 at his home, Parc Farm, one and a half miles north of Dolgellau. After killing her, Jones buried the body in his garden. He then hacked the corpse into 12 pieces and dumped them in the nearby Arran in the hope that they would be washed out to sea. He was hanged at Dolgellau on 23 November 1877. Incidentally, one portion of Sarah's leg was never recovered.

Penrhyndeudraeth: Penrhyn Issa

Even at 68 years of age, miner Thomas Edwards was as strong as an ox. A monster of a man, he was known as 'King of the Mountain'. In the summer of 1812 he was working on repairs to the Great Embankment at Tremadog that had been severely eroded by high seas. With the workers not being paid on time, Edwards began looking enviously at Penrhyn Issa, a farmhouse that stood less than half a mile above one of the embankment's stone quarries. He was sure there was money within those walls. The tenant of the farm was newly-married John Roberts who, on the warm sunny afternoon of 7 September, was out in the fields harvesting, leaving the maid, 18-year-old Mary Jones, alone in the house. Mary was baking bread in the kitchen when Edwards burst in. She made a run for the front door but the big man chased her and, by the entrance, fractured her skull with mighty blows from two stones. He then dragged her back into the house where he slit her throat and stabbed her with shears and a knife. Stealing a watch and two pocket books, one of which contained £35, Edwards made his escape through a back window. He didn't enjoy his new-found wealth for long – he was executed for Mary's murder on 17 April 1813.

SOUTH GLAMORGAN

Gileston Beach

A barren wasteland of rocks and shingle, peppered by a few concrete pillboxes left over from World War II, Gileston Beach was a forbidding place in the depths of winter. On Thursday 29 December 1960, a 14-year-old who lived with his parents at The Cot, a small cottage in the village of Gileston, seven miles west of Barry, went out to play with his friends on the beach less than a mile from his home. He began the walk back alone shortly after 3 pm and was last seen heading towards the grim pillboxes. Soon afterwards a stranger told two girls, who happened to be the boy's sisters, that he had found a boy 'in one of them air-raid shelters up the beachs'. The girls alerted their father who, accompanied by the stranger, found his battered son in one of the pillboxes. He had multiple head injuries caused by blows from a heavy notched stick found nearby. He died later that night from shock and haemorrhage. The stranger was 20-year-old Malcolm Williams, a fitter's mate who worked at the power station at Aberthaw. He had a history of sexual offences against young children. It appeared that Williams had lured the boy into the pillbox on some pretext and, when the boy had resisted his advances, Williams had struck out in anger and frustration. He was found guilty of murder and given life imprisonment. The pillboxes themselves have long gone after the residents of Gileston and St Athan petitioned the local council for their removal. They didn't want any reminders of the murder of an innocent boy.

WEST GLAMORGAN

Brandy Cove, Gower Peninsula

Brandy Cove was the setting for a gruesome find in November 1961 when three pot-holers stumbled upon a dismembered skeleton. Investigations revealed the victim to be Mamie Stuart, a chorus girl who had vanished in 1919 at the age of 26. She had been married to George Shotton with whom she lived. The local postman saw Shotton loading a heavy sack into a van shortly before reporting Mamie missing. But although foul play was suspected, no charges were ever brought since there was no trace of a body. As an added twist, Shotton died in 1958 – three years before the body was finally found.

Swansea: East Pier

When widower James Nash remarried, he kept a secret from his new wife – the existence of his two children. The eldest was away in service so she was no problem but six-year-old Martha was a different matter. Nash had managed to conceal her by placing her in lodgings with a Mrs Goodwin in Plasmarl, Swansea, but he fell 11s 3d in arrears. On the evening of 4 December 1885, Mrs Goodwin confronted Nash outside the Guildhall and said that unless he paid her the money due, he would have to look after Martha himself. It was then that Nash decided to kill his daughter. On that bitterly cold night, he walked Martha down to the East Pier and pushed her into the raging sea below. Her body was recovered from the sea about 80 yards from the pier. Nash received his just deserts at the end of the hangman's rope.

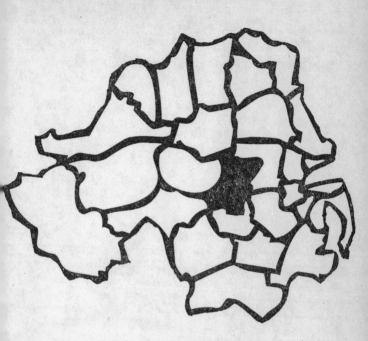

NORTHERN
IRELAND

COUNTY ANTRIM

Seskin, nr Carrickfergus

Twenty-eight-year-old American Eddie Cullins and 26-year-old Turk Achmet Musa had set up an enterprising, if suspicious, money-making scheme. They charged people to see an individual by the name of Zara Agha who they claimed was a 156-year-old native of Asia Minor. The nature of their business meant a great deal of travelling, but that ended on 4 September 1931 when Musa's body was found in a field at Seskin. He had been shot twice in the head and was naked except for a ladies' bathing cap. His blood-soaked clothes were later uncovered in Belfast city centre not far from the hotel where the pair were staying. Cullins was arrested for his partner's murder, found guilty and hanged. Following his execution, a girlfriend of Cullins alleged that the two men were involved in gun-running and that Musa was shot because he had threatened to expose them.

Whiteabbey: Glen House

In the early hours of 13 November 1952, the body of 19-year-old Patricia Curran, daughter of Mr Justice Curran, was found 40 feet from a wooded drive leading to the family home, Glen House. She had been stabbed 37 times and there had been an abortive attempt at sexual assault. Patricia had attended lectures at Queen's University the previous day and when alighting from the

Belfast bus, would usually telephone home for a lift rather than walk up the long, dark drive alone. That evening she made no call, leading police to conclude that she had met someone she knew. Checks at nearby Edenmore RAF Station incriminated 21-year-old Leading Aircraftsman Iain Hay Gordon, a deeply religious young man who knew Patricia's brother and had often visited the house. He was said to have asked fellow airmen for an alibi. Gordon denied the murder at first then made a confession, saying he committed it while in a blackout. At Belfast Assizes in 1953, he was found guilty but insane. However, doubts about his guilt and state of mind persisted and fresh evidence resulted in his acquittal seven years later. The real murderer was never caught.

REPUBLIC
OF
IRELAND

COUNTY CLARE

Cliffs of Moher

The Cliffs of Moher on the west coast near Kilconnell are one of Ireland's most spectacular tourist attractions. But on 24 May 1967 they attracted attention of a different kind when a farmer walking along Doolin Strand at the foot of the cliffs discovered a woman's body. She was American social worker Maria Domenech, the second, but not the last, victim of a twisted love triangle. Maria and her 51-year-old mother Virginia had been having affairs at the same time with suave Patrick D'Arcy, a lady-killer who was to live up to his name. When D'Arcy was no longer able to continue with the double dealing, he decided to kill both women. First Virginia disappeared from her home in New York. Her body has never been found. Then D'Arcy arranged to meet Maria at Orly Airport in Paris from where they flew to Dublin. He hired a car to take them across to the west coast and as they stood admiring the view from the top of the Cliffs of Moher, he threw her over the edge and rifled her handbag. Having wrecked two lives, D'Arcy took his own in a Florida motel room.

COUNTY DUBLIN

Dublin: Phoenix Park

The famous 'Phoenix Park Murders' of 1882 dealt a major body blow to the already shaky Anglo-Irish relations. The killers were members of a newly-formed Irish terrorist group called the Invincibles, whose declared aim was 'the removal of all tyrants from the country'. On 6 May 1882, Lord Frederick Cavendish arrived in Dublin to start his duties as Chief Secretary for Ireland. After a hard day's work in Dublin Castle, he and his Under-Secretary, T. H. Burke, went for an evening stroll in busy Phoenix Park. There they were set upon by four men with long surgical knives and hacked to death. The murderers escaped by driving off in a carriage. Five of the Invincibles were hanged and three others were imprisoned for life after one of their number, James Carey, had turned Queen's Evidence. Following the trial, the authorities tried to smuggle Carey to South Africa but on board the ship he was shot dead by an unknown avenger.

Dublin: Drumcondra

Shoe salesman John Fleming was something of a heel. He had been having an affair with Rita Murtagh, a young waitress at the Dublin restaurant where he lunched every day, but had conveniently omitted to mention that he was married. Indeed he had gone as far as to tell her that he was single and lived with his aunt. So when Rita fell pregnant, she naturally expected Fleming to marry her. In February 1933, the happy couple chose an engagement ring and a wedding ring but Fleming never actually bought them. By 20 July, Rita was growing increasingly restless and told Fleming that she had heard rumours that he was already married. Fleming laughed it off but, with no divorce in Catholic Ireland, he realised he would finally have to kill his wife Ellen. He had been slowly poisoning her since the end of March, feeding her chocolates laced with strychnine, but now the situation called for more drastic action. On the evening of 26 July, with a combination of hammer and fist, 34-year-old Fleming battered his wife to death in the kitchen of their terraced house in the Dublin suburb of Drumcondra. But he had no hope of getting away with murder and was ultimately executed.

Dublin: Leinster Rad, Rathmines

Usually when men murder their wives there is an obvious motive, but in the case of Canadian James Lehman there was none. Lehman lived with his wife Margaret and two children in furnished rooms in Leinster Road, Rathmines, South Dublin. He was a renowned charmer so perhaps he felt that the existence of a wife cramped his style. He told a nurse, with whom he had become friendly, that he and Margaret were not legally married and that her real husband was someone else together. This was of course untrue. At the time, Lehman was running a retail coffee business and was able to buy cyanide from a chemist in Leinster Road on the pretext of testing bottled coffee for sugar. On the evening of Sunday 19 March 1944, he slipped the poison in his wife's rum. Her face turned purple and she died on the way to hospital. Lehman promptly disappeared and evaded capture by using a number of aliases. Eventually he was arrested and charged with murder. Found guilty, he was executed a year to the day after the death of his wife.

Dublin: Green Tureen Restaurant, Harcourt Street

To help pay his expenses, 23-year-old medical student Shan Mohangi worked as a part-time cook at an Indian restaurant in Dublin, the Green Tureen. He also had rooms in the building. His girlfriend was a 15-year-old bank clerk whose mother had forbidden her to marry until she was 17. However, Mohangi was secretly playing the field and came to the conclusion that it was better if his regular girlfriend was out of the way. On 17 August 1963 he took her down to the restaurant basement to show her the cooking equipment. There he strangled her and dismembered the body. He began to burn the head and some of her clothes but the strange smell wafted up to the street above through an iron grille in the pavement. When police searched the premises, they found 17 bodily parts in the storeroom. Mohangi was found guilty of murder but his death sentence was reprieved and he was deported back to his home in South Africa.

Dublin: Phoenix Park

Another Phoenix Park murder in 1982 created almost as much political turmoil as the slayings of Cavendish and Burke. Strapped for cash, Malcolm MacArthur, a graduate of the University of California and son of a wealthy

Irish family, had decided to turn to robbery. In July 1982, he was walking through Phoenix Park on the lookout for a likely getaway vehicle when he spotted 25-year-old nurse Bridie Gargan sunbathing next to her Renault. Using a replica gun, MacArthur forced the terrified girl into the car and when she screamed, he hit her over the head with a hammer, knocking her unconscious. As MacArthur drove off with his wounded victim, an ambulance driver, seeing the hospital sticker on Bridie's car, mistook them for doctor and patient and sounded his siren to help them through the traffic to St James Hospital. Just before the hospital, MacArthur turned off and abandoned the car. Bridie Gargan died four days later. What caused the political uproar was that at the time MacArthur had been a house guest of Irish Attorney-General Patrick Connolly, and was arrested in Connolly's flat. MacArthur pleaded guilty and was sentenced to life.

Ireland's Eye

William Bourke Kirwan was an artist and had used a fair amount of artistic licence to stay married while supporting a mistress, Mary Kenny, who had fathered him seven children! The Kirwans were staying at Howth and on 6 September 1852 they hired a fisherman called Nangle to row them out to Ireland's Eye, the island in Howth harbour. Nangle was told to return for them around 8 pm. An hour before that, screams were heard coming from the island but nobody bothered to investigate. When Nangle arrived at the appointed time, Kirwan was unaware of his wife's whereabouts – he said he had been too busy sketching. The two men searched the island and on a rock at a point known as Long Hole, they found the body of Maria Kirwan lying on a wet sheet, her bathing dress around her neck and cuts on her body. The Coroner's court ruled that death was accidental by drowning but local gossip caused the body to be exhumed and two doctors said that death was from asphyxia. Kirwan was charged with murder and found guilty, the prosecution claiming that he had asphyxiated his wife with a wet sheet to make it look like drowning. Kirwan was released from prison in 1879 whereupon he joined Mary Kenny in the United States of America.

Malahide: La Mancha

The Malahide Mystery of 1926 initially presented itself as one of the most baffling cases in Irish criminal history, but beneath the charred ruins of a gutted house lay the evidence of six cold-blooded murders. La Mancha was a large house standing in its own grounds just off the main road at Malahide, a village outside Dublin, but on the night of 31 March 1926 it was destroyed by fire. Six bodies were found – brothers Peter and Joseph McDonnell (who owned La Mancha), their sisters Anne and Alice and servants James Clarke and Mary McGowan. But the discovery in the passage of a can of paraffin and a candlestick, plus the post-mortem's findings that the three men had died from fractured skulls caused by blows delivered from behind with a heavy blunt instrument, proved conclusively that foul play was afoot. The trail led to the third servant, gardener and family man Henry McCabe. Bloodstained boots and some of Peter McDonnell's clothing were found in McCabe's house. The motive was believed to be robbery. It seems that Clarke was the first to die, attacked from behind by McCabe with a spanner as he bent down to milk a cow.

Then McCabe put a little arsenic into the food of the other five, forcing them to retire to their beds where they were too weak to withstand his violent attacks. Finally he started a number of fires throughout the house in an effort to cover up the crimes. McCabe was found guilty of murder and executed on 9 December 1926.

Shankill: Corbawn Lane

On the morning of 18 February 1936, a bloodstained car was found at the end of Corbawn Lane, Shankill, two miles from the resort of Bray and just 150 yards from the sea. An envelope in the vehicle bore the name of Mrs Vera Ball, a 55-year-old physician's wife, who lived at 23 St Helen's Road in Booterstown, a southern coastal suburb of Dublin. A search of the house revealed blood-stained clothing in the bedroom of her 19-year-old son Edward and it became apparent that mother and son did not see eye to eye. He was charged with her murder although he claimed that his mother had committed suicide with a razor and that he had merely disposed of the body by driving to Shankill and dragging the corpse into the sea at midnight. It seemed more likely that he had hacked her to death with a hatchet. Edward Ball was found guilty but insane. His mother's body, washed out to sea, was never recovered.

COUNTY LIMERICK

Nr Glin: River Shannon

Stephen Sullivan was a devoted manservant to John Scanlan, the Squire of Ballycahane Castle near Limerick. He would do anything that was asked of him – and that included murder. In June 1819 Scanlan, 26, had eloped with and married a local 15-year-old, Ellie Hanley. They honeymooned at Glin on the River Shannon and then moved on to nearby Carrig Island. However, Scanlan quickly began to regret his recklessness in marrying Ellie for she spent money as if it was going out of fashion and did not behave with the decorum required of her position. Scanlan and Sullivan decided the only solution was to get rid of her. Less than three weeks after the wedding, on the moonlit night of 14 July 1819, Ellie was persuaded to go for a late-night trip in a rowing-boat with Sullivan. Four miles off shore, she fell asleep. Fortified by whisky, Sullivan tried to batter her with his shotgun but was so drunk that the first blow crashed down on her shoulder. Ellie woke up in time to see the second blow that shattered her skull. After further attacks, Sullivan removed her clothes (with the exception of her bodice), tied her knees against her chin and threw the corpse overboard, weighted down by a heavy stone. Scanlan told Ellie's friends that she had gone to America but the game was up when the body was washed ashore at Money Point near Glin on 6 September. The arm that Sullivan broke with the first blow was missing and her young head, having provided food for all manner of marine life, was totally devoid of flesh. Scanlan and Sullivan were subsequently hanged.

COUNTY LOUTH

Faughart: Falmore Quarry

Few murders can have had a less compelling motive for their crime than 19-year-old Gerard Toal who killed in order to steal bicycle parts which he then sold to a repair shop. Toal worked as handyman/chauffeur for Father James McKeown, the kindly parish priest in the small village of Faughart near Dundalk. Father McKeown's housekeeper was 36-year-old Mary Callan. On 16 May 1927, Father McKeown was away in Dublin on church business. In the evening Toal collected him at Dundalk station but on their return to the house there was no sign of Mary Cullen or her bicycle. Toal claimed that Mary had told him she was going away but the priest had his suspicions, particularly since she had left all her clothes behind. Eventually, nearly a year later, Father McKeown's new housekeeper found parts from Mary's bicycle in Toal's room above the stables. The Gardai were jolted into action and found Mary's naked body in a sack in the waters of densely wooded Falmore Quarry, some 500 yards from the priest's house. The head and legs had been severed, Toal having once worked for a butcher. Found guilty of murder, Toal was executed on 29 August 1928.

COUNTY OFFALY

Rahan: Ballycloughan

On the death of their mother, brothers Laurence and Bernard Kirwan inherited 70-acre Ballycloughan, a farm some six miles from Tullamore in mid-Ireland. Hardworking Laurence ran the farm, principally because Bernard was in prison for armed robbery. There was bad feeling between the two that continued when Bernard was released on licence in June 1941, for Laurence refused to let him eat at the house. The arrogant and aggressive Bernard was not amused. Then on Saturday 22 November 1941, Laurence failed to keep two appointments in Tullamore and disappeared without trace. Bernard took over the running of the farm, telling one of the workers that his brother had gone to Kildare to look after an aunt's farm. But a neighbour remembered Bernard once attacking Laurence with a knife and remarking afterwards: 'He has escaped me this time, but the next will be a clear cut!' Yet there was no firm evidence of Laurence's fate until 30 May 1942 when the fork of a labourer cleaning the drains in Ballincur bog, about a mile and a half from Ballycloughan, became entangled in a buried sack. The sack contained pieces of human torso. Bernard, who had dismembered pigs at the farm and had worked in the prison butcher's, was charged with murder and executed on 2 June 1943. At his trial, Ballycloughan was aptly described as the 'house of hate'.

COUNTY WATERFORD

Ballyhane: Highways Gate

Young married couple William and Maureen O'Shea lived at the Hill House, a thatched cottage near Ballyhane, a few miles from Cappoquin. It was not a happy union, Maureen particularly objecting to her husband's friendship with 16-year-old Thomas White with whom he frequently played cards until late at night. O'Shea clearly preferred the company of the youth to that of his wife and enlisted White's help in killing her. On 19 February 1943, when O'Shea was out, White started a fire at the cottage. The house was destroyed but Maureen and her baby escaped. On 15 March, O'Shea and White tried again. Armed with the gun issued to him as a member of the Local Defence Force (the Irish equivalent of the Home Guard), White was to lie in wait when the coupled reached Highways Gate on their evening walk. Removing his shoes so that he couldn't be heard, he would creep up from behind and touch O'Shea's shoulder with the gun when he was ready to fire. Sure enough, O'Shea felt the fatal touch and saw his wife shot dead. White was proved to be mentally sub-normal and therefore unfit to stand trial but O'Shea, who had provided the cartridge for the killing and had lured his wife to her death, was found guilty of murder and executed.

SELECT BIBLIOGRAPHY

Encyclopaedia of Murder – Colin Wilson and Patricia Pitman (Pan Books 1984)

World Encyclopaedia of 20th Century Murder – Jay Robert Nash (Headline 1992)

The New Murderers' Who's Who – J. H. H. Gaute and Robin Odell (Headline 1989)

Memories of Murder – Tony Fletcher (Grafton 1987)

Blue Murder? – Joan Lock (Robert Hale 1986)

The Seaside Murders – Jonathan Goodman (Allison and Busby 1985)

The Murders of the Black Museum – Gordon Honeycombe (Comet Books 1983)

Murders After Midnight – Martin Fido (Weidenfeld & Nicholson 1990)

Welsh Murders Volume 1 – Peter Fuller and Brian Knapp (Christopher Davies 1986)

Murder in High Places – Jonathan Goodman (Piatkus 1986)

Crime and Detection – Julian Symons (Studio Vista 1966)

The Black Plaque Guide to London – Felix Barker and Denise Silvester-Carr (Constable and Company 1987)

Such Lethal Ladies – Leonard Gribble (Robert Hale 1985)

Friends and Villains – Tom Roberts (Hodder & Stoughton 1987)

Professor Keith Simpson: An Autobiography (Harrap 1978)

Ill Met By Gaslight – Allan Massie (Paul Harris 1980)

Hampshire Murders – Roger Guttridge (Ensign 1990)

Murder in Lancashire – Alan Sewart (Robert Hale 1988)

Murder in Kent – Philip MacDougall (Robert Hale 1989)

Mac, I've Got a Murder – John McCafferty (Arthur Barker 1975)

The Fingerprint Story – Gerald Lambourne (Harrap 1984)

Cornish Mysteries – Michael Williams (Bossiney 1980)

Famous Cases of Norman Birkett KC – Dennis Bardens (1963)

Murder in the Islands – Sue Simons and Chris Lihou (Redberry Press)

Murders and Mysteries From the Yorkshire Dales – Peter N. Walker (Robert Hale 1991)

The Green Bicycle Murder – C. Wendy East (Alan Sutton Publishing 1993)

ACKNOWLEDGEMENTS

The author would like to thank the following for their invaluable help in the preparation of his book: Aberdeen Journals Ltd, Mr. J. Bennett (Glossop), Cambridge Evening News, Carlisle Library, Chester Library, Cornish Studies Library, Crawley Library, Derby Evening Telegraph, Dundee Courier, Dyfed Archives Service (Pembrokeshire Record Office), C. Wendy East, Essex Police Museum, Evening Chronicle (Newcastle), Glossop Library, Gloucester Citizen, Gloucestershire County Council Local Studies, Great Yarmouth Central Library, Guernsey Library, Gwynedd Archives Service, Paul Harrison, Hereford Library, Huntingdon Library, Kent County Council Local Studies, Kirklees Cultural Services, Liverpool Daily Post & Echo, Leicester Mercury, Leicestershire Record Office, Manchester Evening News, Margate Library, C. S. Middleton, Mitchell Library (Glasgow), Newcastle Chronicle & Journal Ltd., Newport Borough Libraries, The News (Portsmouth), Norfolk County Council Library and Information Service, Nottinghamshire County Libraries, Brian Ollington, Peterborough Evening Telegraph, Geoff Place, Plymouth Library, Rugeley Library, Saffron Walden Library, William Salt Library (Stafford), Scunthorpe Evening Telegraph, Sheffield Star, Shropshire Newspapers Ltd., Southend Library, Suffolk Record Office, Surrey County Records Office,

Tameside Local Studies Library, Warwickshire
County Record Office, Maggie Williams at The
Western Telegraph, Wiltshire County Record Office,
Yorkshire Evening Post and to the editor at Boxtree,
Krystyna Zukowska, for her energy and support.